A LIFE
ROBBED

A LIFE
ROBBED

A LIFE ROBBED

REFLECTIONS ON MY ASYLUM EXPERIENCE IN THE UNITED KINGDOM

FAITH GAKANJE

BROWN DOG BOOKS

First published 2019

Copyright © Faith Gakanje 2019

The right of Faith Gakanje to be identified as the author of this work
has been asserted in accordance with the Copyright, Designs &
Patents Act 1988.

Published under licence by Brown Dog Books and
The Self-Publishing Partnership, 7 Green Park Station,
Bath BA1 1JB

www.selfpublishingpartnership.co.uk

ISBN: 978-1-83952-044-0

Cover design by Kevin Rylands
Internal design by Andrew Easton

This book is printed on FSC certified paper

Printed and bound in the UK

ABOUT THE AUTHOR

Faith Gakanje was forced to seek asylum in the UK in July 2002 to avoid harm and persecution in her home country Zimbabwe. After a series of refusals, her application was finally accepted and she was granted leave to remain in the UK in December 2010. Currently, she is the founder and business owner for Simangaliso designers Zimbabwe and CEO of FaGee Fashions Ltd, an innovative and thriving fashion label that blends African patterns and fabrics with British styles. She is also one of the co-founders and the CEO of the Nottingham African Women's Empowerment Forum (NAWEF), a community interest company predominantly devoted to empowering and championing the rights of women migrants, refugees and asylum seekers of African descent.

An inspirational leader and speaker who has delivered speeches, workshops and seminars on asylum issues and on enterprise development across Europe and Africa, in 2010 she received a Rayne Foundation Fellowship enterprise award to develop FaGee Fashions Ltd. In 2011, she pioneered the "Reunite me with my Children" initiative, following legislation passed by the UK Parliament to stop migrants from uniting with their families. In the same year, she was also included in the list of 100 Women of Substance in Nottingham, a scheme to recognise women who have made a lasting impact on the city.

Faith is a graduate of The Entrepreneurial Refugee Network (TERN) incubator programme and is currently an ambassador for the Family Mentoring Association.

DEDICATION

I dedicate this book:

To my late father, Mr Mangisi Marumisa, you moulded me into an independent, self-reliant woman; you left me when I needed you most.

To my mother Mrs Keresia Marumisa Mhlanga, I have lived the values you instilled in me from my childhood. (Once upon a time, Amai you gave birth to this beautiful woman.) We have had 50 years together and lessons still live. One day soon and very soon we shall meet in the clouds and be together as a big family again. May your soul rest in peace mama.

To my lovely sister Siluzile Marumisa, mother to Patricia and Dallas Dube. You are sadly missed by all of us; we all appreciate your teachings and the skills you passed to us, you left us a sustainable people.

To my brothers, Joseph, Notice & Ephati Marumisa, may your souls rest in peace, I live in hope we will meet up at God's time.

To my grandmother, gogo Kamuchacha Mushonga Marumisa, I kept all your values as a heritage will pass its own.

My grandfather sekuru Marumisa vehushe Nemangwe, your generations continue Mhofu.

Chief Mashame Mhlanga, father to many, my grandfather and great great dad to many generations. May your beautiful soul rest in peace, at 103 years you joined gogo Mugaragumbo my mother's mom. May your souls rest in peace we all miss your presence.

BIOGRAPHY OF FAITH GAKANJE

This book provides a true reflection of Faith's journey through the asylum and immigration system in the United Kingdom. It maps her story, as she struggles to make her way through a heartless and uncompromising immigration and asylum process as practised, that is far removed from the system the UK likes to present across the globe. The book highlighted the passage of a strong and determined woman, coming from a relatively well-to-do, wealthy and privileged background, into a failed system that drove her to the edge of poverty.

Faith Gakanje was born on the 23rd February 1967 in the rural community of Gwehava Village, Gokwe, in the Midlands Province of Zimbabwe. She is the seventh of eleven children born to Chief Nemangwe and Esnath Keresia Marumisa Mhlanga. Her father, Mangisi Marumisa, is one of a dynasty of chieftains belonged to the Korekore ethnic group in Nemangwe clan and part of the Vahera tribe within Gokwe. Growing up, Faith's family owns thousands of acres of farmland, on which they primarily grew cotton and maize. The family also owned a large number of cattle.

As a child, she attended Gwehava missionary school, then went on to study at Amaven Secondary school in Kwekwe, Zimbabwe. After leaving school, she went on to do garment design. As a child of a chief, along with her other siblings, she was groomed to become a leader. Her early childhood leadership training still influences her life today and still remains a critical driving force in her endeavour to achieve. In the 1970s, influenced by her father, a nationalist, at the age of just 11 years, she became a junior girl fighter Chimbwido in Zimbabwe's war of liberation.

Faith matured early, as a strong, independent and self-reliant young woman, and at 17 years she got married and became a mother. In 2002, now a mother of 5 children, due to circumstances that threatened her life, she was forced to flee Zimbabwe, leaving her husband and children, her younger child aged only two years, and to seek sanctuary in the United Kingdom, where she applied for asylum and was rejected five times. As a vibrant, strong and determined woman, one that would leave no stone unturned, she vigorously pursued her goals. In 2006, she took a leading role, along with a number of other ladies, in establishing the Nottingham Africa Women's Empowerment Forum (NAWEF), a platform for supporting and empowering African women, and since then has been a key contributor in community development in the voluntary sector, volunteering for a number of organisation including Save the Children charity shops Nottingham, Rainbow Project Nottingham and the national committee of City of Sanctuary. In 2010, the Home Office finally granted her indefinite leave to remain.

On the 17th of February 2011, Faith was awarded a Rayne Fellowship for refugees, to develop her big idea, a label called FaGee Fashions. The business provides a blend of traditional African designs and fabrics with the current urban trend within the UK. However, two years later, in November 2013, Faith became a widow after the father of her children died.

Faith has since become a graduate of The Entrepreneurial Refugee Network (TERN) incubator programme and is currently Ambassador for the Family Mentoring Association. In October 2016, she qualified under the Common Purpose UK Diaspora Changemakers Leadership Programme. To support the women she works with, Faith is a WRAP (Wellness Recovery Action Plan) facilitator, delivering a wellness toolbox to support women with mental health.

Since Faith gained her indefinite leave to remain, she has been delivering keynote speeches, workshops and seminars on asylum and enterprise issues across Europe and Africa. Her experience and knowledge enable her to speak on women asylum seekers and refugees of African descent.

CONTENTS

FOREWORD

I welcome the opportunity to contribute a foreword to Faith Gakanje's thought-provoking book about her experience with the UK asylum system. Her book has come about at a time when the world is going through an unprecedented refugee crisis. War, violence, persecution and other forms of human rights abuses are driving record numbers of people to be displaced. Although the majority of refugees often seek protection in neighbouring countries, the number who have fled to the UK and other European countries over the past decade has soared.

As a signatory to the 1951 Refugee Convention, the UK has a proud tradition in granting a safe haven to asylum seekers. Faith's experience draws attention to many of the areas where policy makers need to do more to improve the asylum system and make it more welcoming. These include policy issues such as how asylum applications are handled, integration, housing, financial support, legal support, reporting, detention, and how to prevent destitution and homelessness.

Her own experience is reflected in the title of her book. She felt as though the asylum system had robbed her of the best years of her life. After several appeals, it took the Home Office almost nine years to finally accept her asylum application in 2010. She found herself destitute and homeless for much of this period.

GULWALI PASSARLAY
Author of *The Lightless Sky*

ACKNOWLEDGEMENTS

This book would not have been possible without the generous contributions of a large number of people, stakeholders and organisations. They are too numerous to name individually but a number of them deserve a special mention. Firstly, I would like to gratefully acknowledge the contribution of my mentor, Dr Courtney Smith, who helped me to plan and produce the book.

I am also grateful to my compatriot, Morrison Ngwenya, for contributing material to a number of the chapters and for providing moral support.

My brother Kelbert Henriques, thank you for your big heart.

My dear husband, Sunday Adeyemo Ajala, thank you for supporting my vision. You are an amazing soulmate.

During my many years of battle with the UK Authorities to gain asylum, I was helped and supported by a number of amazing people. They shared my sorrow and my joy. Some of them have offered their reflections in Chapters 6 and 7. A special tribute is owed to Trevor Messam, Jonathan Silvery, Dr Olga Bailey, Dr Valerie Howe, Dr Rhoda Madziva, Paul Grant, Professor O.A. Ajala, Kevin Ncube, Deborah Simon author of the bigger picture', Shamsher Chohan, Veronica Barns, Sister Naomi Stewart, Alex Kamanga, Lilleth E Clarke. Mother Patricia Olayinka Abeyeji, chair and core founder of the Global Widows Empowerment Foundation, Fatima Chirara my baby sister, words are not enough – thank you so much, you truly stood by me, Muzukuru Ruvarashe Dumoluhle Mpofu, and my son Takudzwa, thank you for being a good child.

Amdani Juma, you encouraged me to join the voluntary sector simply because you cared for me; you have groomed and natured a leader.

Christopher Harrison, the vicar, and Donna Briscoe-Greene, without your love, encouragement and practical support, I would not have survived my ordeal.

My baby sister, Pauline Edwards, you have done what sisters do, viva you!

Dianne Skerritt, It was hard, my dear sister, (zvakange zvakawoma); you managed my circumstances.

I am also heavily indebted to those who made it possible for me to establish NAWEF and FaGee Fashions. For support with funding and business advice, I would like to single out the Rayne Foundation, TERN, Nottingham City Council and the local National Health Service. Many thanks to Charlie Fraser and Vaughan Jone, former CEO Pyraxis, for all your support to date. I look forward to further building on our partnership.

INTRODUCTION

'No one leaves home unless home is the mouth of a shark, you only run for the border when you see the whole city running as well.'

Warsan Shire

Contrary to popular media narrative, this extract from Warsan Shire's poem reminds us of the grim reality that often forces people to flee their home country. In most cases, it is a life or death decision. It is about personal survival. That was certainly the case for me. In July 2002, fear and persistent threats on my life led me to flee my beloved country, Zimbabwe, for protection in the United Kingdom. This was the most difficult decision I have ever had to make. It meant leaving behind my family (including young children) and friends, a successful business and a lifestyle which was the envy of many. I was brought up in an affluent household in the Midlands province of Gokwe.

My late father belonged to the Korekore ethnic group in *Nemangwe* clan – part of *Vahera* tribe. He was one of a number of chieftains in Gokwe and was called Chief Mangisi Marumisa of Nemangwe. He was a tireless campaigner for equality, freedom and justice for all in our country. At the tender age of 11, I followed in his footsteps and became a member of the country's liberation movement. At the age of 17, I got married and immediately started a family. This was quickly followed by the launch of my first business. I was the proud owner of a profitable textiles business supplying products and services to a wide range of clients, including multinational corporations. During the aftermath of independence in Zimbabwe, my position as a business woman trading with white farmers and business owners placed me on a collision course with the authorities at a time when government policy was to confiscate their property and expel them from the country. At the same time, I also faced domestic unrest and systematic persecution from members of my husband's family.

This book tells my story from life in Zimbabwe to the new and unexpected challenges I faced when I arrived in the United Kingdom. These include the challenges of language, cultural differences, social isolation, homelessness, destitution, misconceptions about asylum-seekers, race and gender discrimination, lack of policies and services to integrate asylum seekers into the host society, and the difficulties of navigating through the United Kingdom's complex and hostile asylum system. My application was rejected four times and it took almost nine years for the Home Office to grant me refugee status. During this time, I was required to move house six times. On one occasion, I was homeless for six months and had to seek shelter in a semi-derelict old police station. The book also discusses the emotional, psychological and mental health impact of the asylum system. It concludes with practical tips to guide asylum-seekers through the asylum process and offers a number of recommendations for improving the asylum system.

The book is motivated by my desire to share lessons from my personal experience to help vulnerable asylum-seekers to better understand the asylum process and to gain timely access to help. At the same time, it is intended to help policymakers to understand the human costs of the asylum system, in the hope that they will reform the system to better meet the needs of traumatised people seeking sanctuary.

Finally, on a more personal note, I also want to use the healing power of writing to make peace with the past and move on to the next phase of my life's purpose with greater focus and optimism. Since gaining the right in December 2010 to settle in the United Kingdom, I have devoted my time and energy to leading the two organisations that I founded – African Women's Empowerment Forum and FaGee Fashions.

As reflected in the title of the book – *A Life Robbed* – I feel as though my life was taken away from me for almost nine years. While I was kept waiting in limbo for the Home Office to make a suitable decision on my asylum application, I could not make firm and meaningful plans to use my skills and experience to help disadvantaged groups. I was not allowed to work or access higher education to use my time wisely. I lived in fear of forcible deportation. I found myself socially isolated, homeless and destitute. My mental and physical health suffered. I had to put the vision for my life and career on hold for years. I felt as though I was robbed of my power and my God-given gifts. I now find myself playing catch-up to achieve goals which I should have achieved a long time ago.

STRUCTURE

The book is organised in three parts with eight chapters. Part One describes life under white minority rule and contains three chapters. Chapter One provides background and contextual information about my village, family structure and childhood years in Zimbabwe. Chapter Two discusses the political climate before independence was granted in 1980 and my role in the liberation movement. Chapter Three discusses the twin challenges of married life, while trying to live in harmony with members of the newly extended family, and running a textile business in a volatile political and economic climate. It provides the context for my decision to seek protection in the United Kingdom.

In Part Two, I discuss my life as an asylum seeker. Chapter Four discusses my hopes and expectations when I fled my country. This is contrasted against the grim reality I encountered in the United Kingdom and my long and protracted battle with the asylum system. Chapter Five discusses the challenges I experienced in accessing public services and integrating into the local community as an asylum seeker. These challenges were made worse by the government's 'hostile immigration environment policy' and the lack of a meaningful integration strategy for asylum seekers and refugees. Chapter Six builds on the previous chapter by discussing how the asylum system contributes to social isolation and mental health problems in asylum-seekers. It also discusses the challenges of living away from my family and friends without appropriate support from the government. My husband passed on soon after I was granted leave to remain.

In Part Three, I discuss the opportunity which refugee status provided. It is an opportunity to make a fresh start and to make up for lost years. Chapter Seven discusses why I set up the Nottingham African Women Empowerment Forum (NAWEF) and FaGee Fashions. As "the voice of the voiceless", this chapter also highlights the impact which NAWEF is having on women's confidence and their general well-being. FaGee Fashions provides a practical example of the entrepreneurial potential of women refugees and how entrepreneurship can help them to take control over their lives. Chapter Eight concludes with the main lessons that asylum seekers and refugees can learn from my experience with the UK asylum system. It also contains recommendations for improving the asylum system so that it can better meet the needs of both the policymakers and people seeking sanctuary.

AUDIENCE

The book is written for a universal audience. There are a host of stakeholders involved in providing services to people seeking sanctuary and in the work to find viable solutions to the global refugee crisis. As a refugee, it is my hope that all of them will benefit from this book, which is based on my first-hand experience with the UK asylum system. They include government bodies, non-governmental organisations, pressure groups, faith organisations, employers, solicitors and the asylum-seekers themselves. Recent estimates put the number of people who have been forced to flee from their country of origin due to conflict, violence and persecution at more than 65 million people.

Given popular misconceptions about asylum-seekers and refugees, the book has an educational value. It will help media interests, policymakers, educational establishments, employers and the public at large to understand why people flee their country of origin, their personal experience, the skills and experience they bring with them, and the contribution they can potentially make to the countries where they are seeking protection.

Faith Gakanje
Nottingham, United Kingdom

CHAPTER ONE

MY CHILDHOOD AND FAMILY LIFE

'Panodya Ishe varanda vanodyawo.' – *'When the chief eats the subjects eat as well.' (i.e. the office of the chief benefits his people)*

Zimbabwean Proverb

This chapter provides background and contextual information about my family structure and childhood years in Zimbabwe.

The name *Zimbabwe* literally means *House of Stone*. It is derived from *dzimba dzamabwe* (great stone houses) or *dzimba waye* (esteemed houses or venerated houses) in the Zezuru dialect of Shona. It dates back to the 12th century. Archaeological findings suggest that the ancestors of modern day Shona people built Great Zimbabwe and hundreds of other smaller stone walled sites in Zimbabwe. These ancient stone ruins of Great Zimbabwe are recognised as a World Heritage site by UNESCO.

Located in Central Southern Africa, Zimbabwe is land-locked and covers an area of 390,580 square kilometres.

It is sandwiched between the Zambezi River to the north and the Limpopo River to the south, and is surrounded by Mozambique, South Africa, Botswana, Namibia, and Zambia. Most of Zimbabwe is rolling plateau, known as *veld*. The country is divided into 10 provinces. The largest province is Mashonaland which covers the eastern two-thirds of the country. Its capital city is Harare. The second largest province is Matabeleland in the west and its capital city is Bulawayo. The third largest province is Midlands. Midlands Province is situated in the centre of the country, roughly equidistant from Harare to the northeast and Bulawayo to the southwest. It stretches from Chiwundura up to Binga Town. It is primarily rural and has an area of 18,300 square kilometres and a population of approximately 500,000 people. The main languages spoken are Tonga, Ndebele and Shona.

According to the latest United Nations estimates in 2018, the country has an estimated population of around 17 million people. The Shona-speaking peoples make up just over 80 per cent of the population and are comprised of the Manyika, Zezuru, Karanga, Korekore, Rozwi, and Ndau groups. They mostly inhabit Mashonaland. The second largest ethnic group is the Ndebele people. They comprise about 14 per cent of the population and they mostly live in Matabeleland, the western third of the country. About 70 per cent of the population live in rural areas. Most of the rest live in Harare and Bulawayo. Zimbabwe made its first commercial relations with Swahili traders on the

Mozambique coast from around the early 12th century and the Shona kingdom became one of Southern Africa's wealthiest and most powerful societies.

My traditional home is in the Midlands province in Gokwe. My late father belonged to the Korekore ethnic group in *Nemangwe* clan – part of *Vahera* tribe. He was called *Chief Mangisi Marumisa of Nemangwe*. My father was one of a number of chieftains in Gokwe. Other prominent chiefs and leaders in the district included *Chireya, Njelele, Tjabi, Pashu, Nkoka, Mashame, Gumunyu* and *Nembudziya*. *Chief Nemangwe* is an inheritance dynasty, a leadership role that is passed down from one generation to another. My father inherited his dynasty from his father who had inherited it from his father, and so on. He was affectionately known as *Machinda*, which means *'the men who surround him and whom he leads'*. As a chief, my father was one of the most influential persons in the region. He oversaw the use of communal land and was in charge of all community affairs. He was the custodian of our customs, traditions, values, language and all aspects of our culture. Members of the community would consult him on any issue that affected them. As a chief he was able to make judgements and hand out penalties. He reported to the government of the day and was the main link between the government and the villagers.

We grew up knowing that the traditional institutions and values, which our people held dearly, had changed in the 1880s when the British arrived with Cecil Rhodes' British

South Africa Company. My mother was my idol. Her name was *Esnath Keresia Marumisa Mhlanga knee Mashame*. She died in October 2018 at the age of 96. Between them, my parents had 11 children and I am the seventh-born child. My mum told me that the land and other resources were owned communally before the whites colonised the country. Land was seen as a gift from *Musikavanhu* (the Creator) God to be used and enjoyed by everyone.

The British colonised the region's land and claimed it as private property, took control of the mineral resources and exploited the population. They disturbed our way of life, introduced their own institutions and laws, criminalised local traditions, disrespected elders and traditional leaders, and angered the ancestral spirits. White people presided over all of our institutions and owned most of the land and other resources in the country. My mother told me that droughts, cattle diseases and other diseases were attributed to the presence of the white invaders. We therefore grew up associating our problems with white people and dreamt of a day when our country would be free from white minority rule.

I was privileged enough to have an almost full primary and secondary school education. This was briefly interrupted by the liberation struggle of the 1970s, which finally led to Zimbabwe's independence in April 1980. Schools were closed for a whole year during the peak of the conflict. Some were destroyed and vandalised as the warring parties thought the enemy was hiding in them. Robert Mugabe's Zimbabwe African National Liberation Army (ZANLA) gained the upper hand in the struggle and his party, Zimbabwe African National Union (ZANU), emerged as the dominant force in the country's post-independence history.

Although women were subordinate to men in this highly patriarchal society, my mother was a very strong and independent woman. She was a large landowner, trader and community midwife *nyamukuta* who was active until her sad passing on in October 2018. We owned in excess of a thousand acres of land.

Thursday was a traditional holiday – *'Chisi'*. One day a week, village people would volunteer to work on our compound for a small reward, usually a bag of maize meal or clothes. We owned huge maize and cotton plantations. We also owned a large herd of cattle. We lived in a large house, which was made from concrete blocks, stone materials and zinc roofing. Most of the houses in the village were made from mud, wattle, sun-dried bricks and thatched roofs. In a separate building, we had a large kitchen with seats for up to several dozen people, even though it was customary for women to sit on the floor.

Mealtime was very important in our household. Food was eaten communally from a large dish or bowl while sitting on the floor in a circular formation. We were taught to wash our hands before eating and always to eat with our right hand (*rudyi*). Our staple diet was a cornmeal-based dish called *Sadza*. This could be prepared in a number of ways and was usually eaten with meat and vegetable stew, and mashed beans (*rupiza*). Fruits and vegetables of all types were abundant and cheap. Beef and meat from antelopes and wild animals were readily available. Caterpillars (*madora*), *mopane* worms, a variant of *madora*, and flying ants (*ishwa*) were usually on the menu. We would also share the birds, which we hunted with catapults and snares. These would be eaten roasted or fried on open-air wood fires. It was forbidden to eat the meat of our clan's totem or any type of food that bore their family name. Our totem is *Chihera*.

I was born on 23rd February 1967 in Gokwe district, Gwehava Village. I grew up in Rhodesia under white minority rule. My parents named me *Fungai Rutendo Marumisa*. I was given a Christian name, Faith, at the age of 6 when I began to attend *Gwehava* missionary school, a primary school established by the Methodist church. This was routinely applied to anyone who did not have a western name or who had a name which the whites considered 'strange' or difficult to pronounce. I was allowed to keep my other traditional names. *Marumisa* literally means 'take a deep bite' and *Gakanje* is my married name,which means 'crab'.

Women were encouraged to eat eggs to boost their fertility. Milk from cows was widely available. Goat milk was often given to sick children as it was believed to contain healing properties. For special family gatherings and other ceremonial occasions, my mother used to make *Seven Day* beer from grains grown on our land. She sold her fermented beer in the local market. This beer was very strong – it was brewed over seven days, as implied by the name. Sometimes my father and his friends would stay up all night and travel from house to house drinking *Seven Day* beer. His return home intoxicated the next day often resulted in bitter arguments with my mother. She was a very strong woman who earned the nickname *Vapashuwa* – meaning someone who stands for truth.

From a very young age, my mother instilled in me the same values of equality, self-sufficiency, hard work, truth, justice and resilience which defined her. My mum believed the woman is the fabric of society and is the one who expands the world, hence the saying *musha mukadzi*. In our culture the expression literally means 'a single man cannot establish a home on his own'. As children of a chief and an affluent family, we were groomed from an early age to become leaders. Although we had domestic helpers and help from members of the extended family, we were still expected to do household tasks to make us well rounded. These included learning to cook, clean, tend to the garden and help on the farm.

These values were further reinforced by my grandmother. I was frequently compared to her. She was a very wise woman and was affectionately called *Kamchacha* translated as the '*cleverest one*' or '*God's anointed one*'. Many people saw her as a witch-doctor – *n'anga* or *mufemberi* – as she had the gift to heal people and to interpret dreams and signs. I spent a lot of my childhood years with her. She had a huge influence on my life. She taught me to be strong and to believe in myself. I remember with fondness the countless hours she spent educating me into the virtues of self-identity. She was saddened by the impact of colonialism and white minority rule on our indigenous culture. The white population introduced values and practices which conflicted with our way of life and brought about greed and divisions in Zimbabwean society.

Musha makadzi (the three legged pot), mutsvairo/broom, Ngoma/drum, ne pfuko

One such practice was family and birth control. This was viewed as barbaric because it was meant to control the growth of the black population. They injected women with the same drug used for animal contraception. This produced harmful side effects such as changes in menstrual periods, heavy bleeding, headache, stomach cramp and dizziness. She told me she had witnessed women bleed to death. Her dream was to expel the colonialists and regain control of our country. She often invoked spiritual rituals in the struggle to free the country of white minority rule. Her strong sense of justice left a lasting impact on me. This was what influenced me to become a junior girl fighter *Chimbwido* in the war to liberate Zimbabwe in the 1970s. I was only 11 years old when war broke in our village.

My parents loved all their children but I am in no doubt that I was the apple of their eyes. There were eleven siblings – four boys and seven girls. We were known as the '*golden girls*'. I was the youngest girl and my position as seventh gave me pride of place. As a young child I did not understand the fascination with the number seven. I have since found out that seven is regarded as a 'perfect and sacred number' in many religions and cultures. It is no wonder there are seven days in a week, seven colours of the rainbow, seven seas in the world, seven Wonders of the World, and so on. Even as a very young girl, my father valued my opinion and often sought my advice in many of the cases he presided over as a tribal chief and a custodian of justice. He often invited me to the local court – *dare remachinda* – to listen and observe the trials. One of my sisters and three of my brothers are now deceased.

This privilege was not given to my other sisters. I remember in one divorce hearing, he asked me for my thoughts on how the assets owned by the couple should be shared. Decisions were often made by local custom rather than by parliamentary laws. It was customary for the man to get the major share of the assets in divorce settlements. On this occasion, I advised that equal shares of the property should be given to the man and woman. This meant an equal number of cattle. In an economy based on agriculture and livestock, ownership of cattle gives a person status. I wanted to see women empowered and treated fairly.

My father respected my views and always took it into account in his final judgment. Like my mother, he was also keen that I receive a very good education. They used to say that one day I would become a doctor or an air hostess. In those days an air hostess was seen as a person with status, power and fame. People thought air hostesses lived a life of luxury, globe-trotting and indulging in leisure.

I had my own views of what I wanted to become. It was customary for girls to follow in their mother's footsteps and for boys to adopt their father's roles. I was no different. I wanted to be a midwife (*nyamukuta*) like my mother. Much of her training was based on oral tradition and knowledge of natural remedies handed down from one generation to another. My mum knew how to deliver babies safely and to make the women comfortable and pain-free. She recalled with horror how one of my aunts had died while she was giving birth, due to the lack of proper healthcare facilities. She had died on her way to hospital while she was in a scotch-cart – pulled by cattle or donkeys – as there were no ambulance facilities.

My dear mother her final farewell @ Claybank in Gweru hospital October 2018, surrounded by my siblings. Left to right: Shelly Siziba, Fatima Chirara and Betty Matumo

Besides being prepared for employment, the girl child was also expected to be a good wife and homemaker. Girls were brought up to be obedient wives. They were taught to cook, wash, iron, clean, honour and serve their husbands.

In general, they were not socialised to become professional people as well. By the age of twelve, a girl was expected to be a competent home-maker. Home was a testing ground to demonstrate you had developed and honed all these skills.

In Zimbabwe, some girls get married very young by western standards. Teenage marriage is particularly prevalent in the rural areas and among the poorer segment of the population. The constitution allows girls to get married from age 16. However, girls can get married at a younger age depending on personal preference, the local custom and religion. There is no minimum age of marriage under the Customary Marriages Act. It is still common for children to be pledged into marriage, even though there are now laws which forbid forced marriage. I was just over 16 when I got married. My last day at school was on 6th December 1984 and I got married less than three weeks later on 25th December. At least I finished my education before I got married and started a family. I was not forced to get married when I did. My sisters got married at a younger age and their education was never treated as a priority. Unlike me, three of them did not attend secondary school. Nowadays there are various civil society campaigns to end child marriage.

I resumed my primary school education after the war ended in 1980, the year in which President Mugabe introduced a number of long overdue reforms to the education system. Education was declared a basic human right and the constitution was changed to make primary and secondary school education free and compulsory. Today

Zimbabwe boasts one of the highest adult literacy rates in Africa. Children are entitled to 13 years of primary and secondary school education over a school year spanning 40 weeks. Long before these reforms were introduced, my father founded his own schools in our village and surrounding areas to help his people. I went to one of the primary schools in the village where I was born. This school was a short walk from my home, no more than five minutes.

I spent four years at secondary school, where my time was more challenging. I attended *Amaveni* Secondary School in the city of *Kwe Kwe*, nearly 150 kilometres from my village. One of my sisters also attended this school at the same time as me. The biggest challenge was living apart from my parents for long periods. We were boarded in a hostel during term time and would return home during the holiday periods.

I have very fond memories of my school days. I was a fast learner and was top of my class. I particularly excelled in mathematics and the science subjects. I was left-handed and this was considered to be taboo. The left hand was referred to as the 'wrong hand', the 'devil's hand' and the 'unclean hand' used to wipe the bottom after defecating. My teachers forced me to use my right hand for tasks which I would normally perform with my left hand. Each time I used my left hand to write or eat they would beat me with a cane or punish me in other ways. I had no choice but to learn to write with my right hand.

At school, as well as in academic subjects, I was also

good at sport. I was one of the best netball players. I was also an outstanding bottle racer. This involved running as fast as you could whilst balancing a bottle on your head. I won many prizes and my parents were very proud of me. I felt empowered from a very young age. My parents also taught me to defend myself if anyone did anything to hurt me. I was encouraged to take responsibility for my life, solve problems for myself as far as possible and to be self-sufficient. I remember crying and complaining to my mum on one occasion after another child at school had bullied me. She reprimanded me strongly and sent me back to school to face the bully and demand an apology. He apologised unhesitatingly when he noticed the intent for revenge in my eyes. From that day on I was left in peace.

As part of growing up, I participated in a variety of cultural and traditional children's play-times. Outside of school play-time was made up of so many memorable games and activities. I spent most of my time playing with my brothers and sisters. The games we played depended upon our age and gender. Among the games played was *matakanana* or *mahumbwe* (playhouse). In this game children would role-play adult roles. The boy would take on the role of the father while the girl took the role of the mother. *Chamuvandemuvande* (hide and seek) was another of the popular games played by everyone. Someone would go and hide. They would make a sound to signal to others to search for them. This game sharpened searching skills. *Amai Ndakanaka*, meaning 'Mother I am very beautiful' was commonly played among girls. Boys enjoyed playing games that mimicked war. *Sunga musoro wedendende* was played by both boys and girls. This is a game in which you pick the one who you consider to be beautiful or special.

Another common pastime in my village was dancing. Dancing served many purposes and there were different types of dance depending on whether the purpose was religious, social or ceremonial. I was taught *Shangara*, *Kwasa Kwasa*, *Jerusarema*, *Muchongoyo and* other traditional dance genres at home and later at primary and secondary schools. Dancing was used to teach moral values, pass on ancient customs and traditions, communicate with ancestral spirits and celebrate significant events. It was also seen as a form of physical activity and a way of attracting members of the opposite sex.

We were expected to uphold my father's standing in the community and to be well behaved at all times. From the oldest to the youngest, we were the custodians of the traditional values which had been handed down to us over the years. We were brought up to serve our community. On weekends, we would volunteer to clear paper and other rubbish from the grounds of our local school. I was deeply inspired by the motto at my primary school: 'Ever Onwards – Knowledge is Power'. It taught me to value education. I saw first-hand the type of problems that could happen if one could not read and write. I can remember a young lady who had to rely on someone to read and write letters for her. Her boyfriend did not know she could not read and write. She had a friend who would do this for her. She ended up losing her boyfriend to her friend. Her friend would write the opposite of what she asked her to write. Out of jealousy, tender sentiments such as 'I love you' were deliberately changed to 'I don't love you anymore.'

Gwehava mission primary school

Apart from the games we played, we were taught important life skills and lessons through stories told by elders. For example, we were told that if we sat in the road we would get huge boils and sores on our bums. This was their way of telling us to avoid danger and stay safe. Nowadays it would be danger from motor vehicles. Back in the 1970s when I was a child, vehicles in the village did not exist in large numbers. My grandfather was one of the few people with motor vehicles. He was a prison guard. The source of danger was more likely to come from carts, animals, *mondao* (mermaids) and angry ancestral spirits. The punishment for breaking the rules was harsh. Girls were generally punished by their mothers and boys by their fathers. My mum would withhold food from us for long periods. Sometimes we would be flogged with a hard belt as well, depending on the severity of the misdemeanour.

Belief in *tokoloshis* (ghosts) was widespread. Spirits were both feared and revered. We were told they had the power to harm us or to give us prosperity depending on whether or not they were pleased with our behaviour. Incidents such as death of a child, illness, disability, people going missing, drought, poor harvests and other misfortunes were usually attributed to the influence of spirits. Stories abound of mermaids luring people to their death. It was believed they lived in the dams, lakes and reservoirs. They would enchant their victims to the bank of rivers and drag them into the deepest sections of the water or pull them under the waves to their death.

Sometimes this would prevent us from going about our normal activities. There have been many reported sightings of mermaids at Gwehava/Sengwa dam near my home. Fishermen have been chased away whenever they try to catch bulk fish for resale. Interestingly, in 2012 repair work on the Gokwe dam was ceased because of terror from mermaids. People mysteriously vanished and workers were chased by mermaids. The same happened when the government brought in white workers at premium fees. Workers refused to return to work. Things only calmed down when the Rural and Urban Development Minister, Ignatius Chombo, arranged with the tribal chiefs of the area to perform rites and rituals to appease the mermaids and other evil spirits.

As chief of the area, this was one of my father's responsibilities. In the month of August, after the main harvest, animals would be slaughtered under a huge tree. Every drop of blood would be carefully collected in a bucket and left overnight under the tree for the spirits to drink. It is widely believed that our ancestors who built Zimbabwe still live there. For this reason the nationalist movement promoted Zimbabwe as a sacred place, even though this was played down by the colonial powers. It was common for tribal chiefs and the *ngangas* or *masvikiro* (traditional healers) to call on the ancestral spirits to help us during the war. Many people believe the country would be still under colonial rule had it not been for the help received from the spirit world. During the liberation struggle in the 1970s, it was common to kill political enemies and dispose of their bodies in the dams and rivers. This is another reason why dams, reservoirs and boreholes are considered to be haunted places.

My father became a born-again Christian before he died. He replaced many of his traditional spiritual rituals with Christian practices. He was baptised in the Apostolic Church and became a deacon and evangelist. Although he was not able to read before his conversion, miraculously he taught himself to read the Holy Bible and preached the gospel throughout the whole Gokwe district. Many people were converted to Christianity as a direct result of his preaching and ministry. He became humbled by his conversion and refused to place any importance on his standing as a chief. The other members of my family also converted to Christianity. Church attendance, praying and singing was a major part of our family life. Before my parents died, they encouraged us to remain united as a family and to show love and respect to everyone. These values became part of me for the rest of my life. I have become who I am today because I was groomed from an early age to love myself and to be strong and resilient when faced with challenges.

CHAPTER TWO

MY LIFE AS A JUNIOR FIGHTER CHIMBWIDO

'A man who makes trouble for others is also making trouble for himself.'

Chinua Achebe

This chapter discusses my role as a junior girl fighter *Chimbwido* in the struggle to free my country from white domination and colonial exploitation.

From a very young age, I was exposed to guerrilla warfare and civil unrest. The words guerrilla warfare *hondo ye Chimurenga* (popularly known as *Chimurenga war*), seemed to make their way into almost every conversation in our household. It was often the topic of conversation on the streets and in the meetings which my father conducted. Guerrilla warfare is a form of irregular warfare in which a small group of combatants, such as paramilitary personnel, armed civilians, or irregulars, use military tactics including ambushes, sabotage, raids, petty warfare, hit-and-run tactics and mobility to fight a larger and less-mobile, traditional military. It was a struggle to liberate Zimbabwe from white domination. Every black Zimbabwean played a role in this struggle. Women often fought alongside men but children helped the guerrilla army in whatever way they could. We boosted morale by singing during night gatherings, cooked for the fighters and were sent on errands to spy on the enemy. Even though I was only 11 years old, I played my full part in that struggle for independence. And for that reason, I am very proud. The background to this uprising should be taken into account. The aim was to end oppression and domination from foreign occupation and reclaim our country for our people. This was a cause worth dying for. In the late 19th century, the British arrived in Zimbabwe with Cecil Rhodes' British South Africa Company (BSAC) and disturbed our communal way of living. Rhodes and the settlers who invested in his company had hoped to find large deposits of gold and other precious minerals. When this failed to materialise, investors were compensated with large tracts of land. Land which had previously been held communally for the benefit of everyone in a given chiefdom was now pillaged as private property and allocated to European immigrants.

Cecil John Rhodes and his BSAC restructured the land they had grabbed. The area between the Limpopo River to the south and the Zambezi River to the north was named Southern Rhodesia and the region to the north was named Northern Rhodesia (modern day Zambia) after 1898 in honour of Cecil Rhodes. Southern Rhodesia was further divided into regions. Our people were pushed to the infertile areas while white settlers occupied prime land. The country was divided into five farming zones, loosely corresponding to rainfall patterns. The best land was concentrated in zones 1, 2 and 3, where the rainfall was high. Land in these areas was suitable for cultivation of crops such as maize, wheat and tobacco. Zone 4 was suitable for livestock and crops which needed little rainfall. Zone 5 was low veld and prone to drought. Land ownership in these zones was determined by race. The first three zones were reserved for white settlement under the provisions of the Southern Rhodesia Land Apportionment Act, passed in 1930. Zone 5 (and a part of Zone 2 with rainfall variability) was organised into the Tribal Trust Lands and was exclusively reserved for blacks. Although making up less than 1% of the population, it is estimated that white Zimbabweans owned more than 70% of the arable land prior to 1980.

Despite the setback suffered by the natives in the 1896–97 revolt, they did not give up in their quest to drive the colonialists out of our country and regain control over our resources. Land hunger was a major source of friction. Our people were robbed of their land and struggled to find land to graze their livestock and produce crops. Alongside this deprivation, vast swathes of land were left idle under white ownership as a result of the system of land tenure created by the white minority government.

Historically, there were three phases to the Chimurenga wars. Phase one was conducted in the late 1890s. This was when the Ndebele and Shona people waged war against the administration set up by the British South Africa Company. This war was waged by unarmed spiritual traditional leaders like mbuya Nehanda, Kaguvi and others who faced their death by hanging. Phase two of the Chimurenga war took place during the 1960s up to 1979. It was fought between African nationalist guerrillas against the mainly white Rhodesian forces. It was a resistance to colonial oppression. Phase three came about after 1979 and was about land reform. This phase witnessed an extensive process of repossession and redistribution of land from the white minority to the indigenous population. The land reform issue still remains, despite many land reform programmes since independence was gained in 1980. The land reform programme was implemented to redistribute land equitably. Some farmers who had large expanses of land, lost land to the government's 'willing-buyer-willing-seller' programme. White farmers who owned more than three farms were forced to sell under this programme. This phase of land redistribution left some white farmers disgruntled and they resisted the government programme of land redistribution.

Apart from the skewed distribution of land along racial lines, there were other problems inherent in this system. The lack of individual title in areas designated as Tribal Trust Lands hindered the development of the land through soil improvement, grading, irrigation, drainage and roads. It is also reported that some white farmers were guilty of encroaching on land set aside for black settlement. In some cases, they shifted their land boundaries into land reserved for black farmers.

As Ian Douglas Smith, the Prime Minister, experienced pressure from African leaders who demanded full control of their land, he came up with a new constitution in the 1960s which was meant to provide Africans with some limited participation in the administration of the government and to redress the land issues that did not satisfy African leaders. For the first time, the traditional leaders were recognised as the final authority for all matters relating to land held in trust for the natives under the Tribal Trust Lands scheme. This was not enough to satisfy our people. We wanted to see African majority government and an end to colonial rule, and to regain control over our land and other resources. African majority government was already a reality in neighbouring Zambia and Malawi by 1953 when the Federation of Rhodesia broke up. Although Britain wanted to see the same in Rhodesia, Ian Douglas Smith refused to cooperate. On November 11, 1965, he unilaterally declared Rhodesia's independence from Great Britain.

As the white regime tightened its grip over our people, black opposition to minority rule grew. By the 1950s and 1960s, a new generation of freedom fighters emerged. They were better organised and had a clearer strategy to challenge the injustice and end white minority rule. Political parties and military organisations were established. In 1961, the Zimbabwe African People's Union (ZAPU) was formed, led by Joshua Nkomo. Its military wing was Zimbabwe

People's Revolutionary Army (ZIPRA). The party later split over tribalism and disagreement on tactics of how best to overthrow the colonial regime. The split resulted in the launch of the Zimbabwe African National Union (ZANU) in 1963 under Robert Mugabe and a revolutionary wing known as the Zimbabwe African National Liberation Army (ZANLA).

ZAPU was organised as a Marxist–Leninist political party, while ZANU was based on Chinese Maoist political ideology. Support to both parties followed tribal lines. ZAPU drew its support mainly from the Ndebele tribe and ZANU's support came primarily from the Shona people. ZANU's ideology relied on mechanisms to politicise the villagers and gain their support in the liberation struggle. Bases and camps were established near villages so that the villagers would provide the guerrillas with food, shelter and other provisions. Both parties were banned by the Rhodesian authorities.

Both parties mounted sustained guerrilla campaigns against Ian Douglas Smith's government throughout the 1970s until independence was finally granted in 1980. ZANLA had combatants throughout the country for guerrilla fighting as well as in Mozambique, while ZIPRA mounted opportunistic strikes from its bases in Zambia and Angola.

Although both parties and their military wings often fought against each other whilst working to free the country from white minority rule, they were equally subject to the same ruthless treatment by the Rhodesian government. Both forces recorded huge losses at the hands of the Rhodesian security forces. The war intensified from the mid-1970s. Both groups of guerrillas mounted successful strikes in the cities and frequently disrupted the physical and communication infrastructure. Farms belonging to whites and isolated government buildings, including schools and healthcare facilities, were vulnerable to attacks. Military operations were also waged in the regions designated as Tribal Trust Lands. Large areas of land were left idle as farmers fled for safety.

Both ZAPU and ZANU mobilised women and children to become involved in the liberation war. Although I was still only a child, I remember very well the call from ZANU under the popular slogan 'Liberation through Participation'. Thousands of women responded to the call. It is estimated that 25–30% of ZANLA's liberation army was made up of women at the time of independence. Women were a major force in the liberation struggle because it was a means of liberating themselves not just from colonial domination but also from male domination. Their role was to cook and manage strategies to sustain the boys, commonly called comrades, *Vakomana,* in the bush. The regime called them terrorists because they caused terror across the country.

My own dream was to see my country liberated and live in a stable and prosperous society where all women were empowered to reach their full potential. I was prepared to do my part, no matter how small. I was encouraged by my grandmother. She despised the white invaders who plundered our resources and undermined our traditional way of living. She was worried that our children would soon disrespect their parents and elders. It was customary for us to kneel and bow when we greeted elders. The white settlers had no respect for these values. My mum also supported my decision to participate in the struggle. My father was less enthusiastic. He was worried that I might be abused by the male guerrilla fighters and lose my virginity. If a woman was not a virgin when she got married, her family would have to pay compensation to her husband. If the man who took her virginity was known, the woman's family would try to demand this compensation (damage) from him or his family.

Although there were reports of girls and women who had been abused by the guerrilla fighters, these were isolated cases. For the most part, they were disciplined fighters who were taught to respect women. Those who behaved badly towards women were subject to harsh punishment. Violence towards women was more likely to be conducted by the Rhodesian soldiers.

When the war reached my village in 1978, I was only 12 years old. I thought about all the reasons why I should take part and I was left in no doubt that it was a cause worth dying for. We stood to lose our land, our dignity and our basic freedoms. I decided to take a stand against injustice, racism and colonial oppression. Like many of my country folks, I could have tolerated the presence of the colonialists if they had acted reasonably and shown respect for our country. I detested the fact that they created classes and other divisions in my country. There were areas where blacks could not enter.

The 1930 Land Apportionment Act was designed to segregate whites from blacks. Only whites were allowed to own land in the urban areas. Although by then urban blacks far outnumbered whites, they were often forced to live in rented accommodation located miles from city centres. Curfews were often set up and any black person seen in the prohibited areas during the curfew hours was often beaten and even killed without any recourse to justice. Areas like central Salisbury were almost exclusively reserved for whites. It was common for large numbers of black people to go missing. Women had no rights to vote. They did not even own any form of identification card that was legally recognised. There was no equality between the sexes. It was worse for black women as they were also subject to racism under the white minority government in our own country. I became a bitter and angry little girl listening to such practices of injustices.

I would stop at nothing short of complete liberation of my country from white minority rule. Most people joined the struggle out of a sense of patriotism. For the most part, they joined voluntarily, although there are accounts of people who were kidnapped to take part in the war. A notable account is the so-called kidnapping of hundreds of school children by ZIPRA from the Manama Mission School. The Rhodesian leader sent buses to Botswana to take the children back home but they refused to board the buses and insisted on going to the camps to train as freedom fighters.

This incident was a turning-point as it encouraged many

people to cross the border to Zambia to join the struggle. The view expressed by one villager, Comrade Frank Dube, was shared by many people: *'It was unfortunate that I was not anywhere close to Manama when it happened but if I was around I would surely have joined them because during that period this is what everyone was talking about — joining the liberation struggle.'*

Chimbwido junior fighter

Children who crossed the border to Zambia and other surrounding areas to take part in the war were often put in schools whilst learning about the art of warfare and the history of that country. Although I was not trained in warfare and did not have the physical strength to fight alongside men, I found ways to help the guerrilla fighters from my home. My cooking skills were as useful as my ability to fight. My grandmother and mother taught me to cook all our traditional dishes from a very tender age. My new mission was to ensure the guerrillas had food, water, clothes, shelter and any information or intelligence I could pass on to them about the enemy. My brothers also participated in the war. My sisters were living in the city so they were not involved.

Soldiers from the white South African army would often call from house to house looking for guerrilla fighters. It was not uncommon for them to come with bribes in the form of food as they eagerly asked, 'Did you see the boys around here?' I was taught to keep secrets. Of course, my answer would be a firm 'No', even though I often knew exactly where in the bush they were hiding. They told me their hiding place as it was where I was required to bring their food, water and other provisions.

I also helped the guerrilla fighters by giving them information about the movements of the white Rhodesian army and their allies. When the Government forces brought bribes in the form of food to persuade us to disclose the whereabouts of the guerrilla fighters, we accepted the food the enemy brought us but we did not eat it and we did not give it to our guerrilla fighters. It was rumoured the food contained poison as the white people wanted to get rid of us and we had to fight the enemy for our role to be recognised. As Tanya Lyons points out in her book, *Guns and Guerrilla Girls: women in the Zimbabwean liberation struggle*[1], we simply could not trust them. Stories abound of local people who had died or become gravely ill after eating contaminated food from the Rhodesian forces.

During the war, I remember leading a group of young people in our village, to raise awareness of the work that would be effective in advancing the cause of freeing our country from white domination and colonial rule. Gathering in a circle, we used to sing and dance songs of victory for hours with our fists clenched as a sign of overcoming the racist Smith regime. This was even before we had won the war. I favoured a song called ZANU Chiwororo – which literally meant our party was the champion of champions and one day we would be celebrating our independence.

During all gatherings, we would chant 'Viva Chimurenga' and 'Viva ZANU' and that became our motto. I was prepared to die for the cause of liberating my country. I encouraged a lot people of my age to stay engaged and be strong until we reached our goal. As a sign of dedication to the struggle, I included this wish in my will epitaphs: *kana ndafa muhondo paguva rangu munyore kuti 'Mafaro nemorari'*. This literally means 'When I die during this war, on my grave you write meaning happiness.' I was strong and fearless. I drew inspiration from *Cry the Beloved Country*, a radical book written during the Apartheid era in South Africa by Alan Paton[2]. This book taught me about promoting the voice of the voiceless, the empowerment of nations, what people can do to empower themselves and how to gain freedom. I was also inspired by other revolutionary works and songs. These included the song 'My Mother land' from Yvonne Chaka Chaka.

I am glad to see that the role of children and women in the liberation struggle is now receiving the prominence it deserves. For a long time the role of women in the liberation struggle went unrecognised. This can easily happen in a society where men wield all the power and women are expected to accept their role in the home as bearers of children and serving men's needs. However, in recent years, efforts are being made to re-write our country's history and to give full recognition to the major role which women played in the war to secure the country's independence. An excellent account of women's contribution to the liberation war is provided in the Tanya Lyons' book, mentioned above. It is now common to talk about the 'mothers of the revolution'.

CHAPTER THREE

FAMILY AND BUSINESS LIFE IN A TURBULENT
CLIMATE

This chapter discusses the twin challenges of married life
while trying to live in harmony with members of the newly
extended family, and running a textile business in a volatile
political and economic climate. It provides the context for
my decision to seek protection in another country.

This is an admission that you did not have to cross
the border to Zambia or Mozambique to learn to use a
ar pervaded the whole country. It came even to the most
remote village.

Canaan Sodindo Banana, who served as the first
President of Zimbabwe from 1980 to 1987, described
women's participation in the war as the greatest equaliser
of the sexes:

*'The women combatants, peasant mothers and young
girls ... clearly demonstrated that women should never be
underestimated. The women cadres fought side by side
with their male counterparts, displaying the same spirit of
determination and courage until final victory. In the rural*

areas, peasant women brushed aside threats of reprisals from the Smith regime and threw all their weight behind the armed revolution. They protected our gallant freedom fighters, nursed the wounded and fed the hungry. Even little girls were also in the forefront of the war. As Zvimbwido the young girls showed you unbreakable determination and revolutionary spirit by transporting equipment for the comrades, by mobilising the population and providing vital intelligence on enemy manoeuvres. The war was thus won through concerted action by both men and women. There was total unity in action.[3]

The war produced huge casualties for all the warring factions. Although estimates vary considerably, it is often said that some 20,000 people lost their lives during the conflict, more than half of whom were guerrilla fighters. Rhodesian security forces often carried out punitive raids on villagers accused of aiding guerrilla fighters. Many were also victims of cross-fire, land mines, air attacks and commando raids on guerrilla camps in Zambia and Mozambique. No one was spared from the atrocities. Murders of women, children and missionaries were widely publicised. The war also disrupted economic activities and public services. Farmers were killed in some cases. Farms were destroyed. Veterinary services were disrupted. All of this resulted in a drop in agricultural and livestock production.

The war came to an end on 21 December 1979 following the signing of the Lancaster House Agreement by the warring parties in London. The leaders of ZANU (Robert Mugabe) and ZAPU (Joshua Nkomo) sent a joint delegation called the Patriotic Front (PF). Direct British rule was temporarily introduced to nullify Rhodesia's minority rule and to govern the country until elections took place in February 1980.

The elections were won by Robert Mugabe's party with the votes split along tribal lines. All but three of the sixty seats in the heavily populated Shona areas went to ZANU-PF and the twenty seats in the Ndebele stronghold of Matabeleland went to ZAPU-PF. The country was declared independent on 18 April 1980 with Robert Mugabe as its first Prime Minister. In a government of national unity, Nkomo was appointed as Minister of Home Affairs in his 22-member Cabinet. A further three Cabinet posts were given to ZAPU members and three to white ministers. This included General Peter Walls, previously the Rhodesian armed forces commander. He was appointed as military chief. Ken Flower was retained as Head of the Central Intelligence Organisation. Ironically, during the Smith regime, Flower's overriding remit was to get rid of Mugabe. Various assassination attempts were made on his life to no avail. Mugabe also developed a close relationship with Ian Smith, the former Rhodesian leader, much to everybody's surprise. This was the man who had thrown him in prison for eleven years and even denied him parole to attend the funeral of his only child at the time.

In his first television address in 1980, Mugabe made clear his intention to unify the country and to move on from the country's bitter past. He told the nation, 'We will ensure there is a place for everyone in this country ... I urge you, whether you are black or white, to join me in a new pledge to forget our *grim past, forgive others and forget, join hands in a new amity and together as Zimbabweans trample upon racism.'*

Mugabe did not want to make the same mistakes that newly independent African countries Mozambique and Tanzania had made. These economies collapsed when their Marxist-inspired leaders nationalised and collectivised their industries. The whites migrated in large numbers and took their capital and expertise with them. For this pragmatic reason, white Zimbabweans were re-assured that they had nothing to fear. Mugabe realised the stability and prosperity of the new Zimbabwe depended on the continuing investment and co-operation with the government of the whites. They were offered generous incentives and protection. For the first few years after independence, many white farmers and business owners commended his policies and even addressed him as *'Good old Bob'*[4].Some white Rhodesians who had previously fled even returned to help build the new Zimbabwe. At the same time, they were worried by some of the symbolic changes he had introduced. The name Southern Rhodesia was disbanded and replaced with Zimbabwe. Likewise the name of the country's capital was changed from Salisbury to Harare. Cecil Square was renamed Africa Unity Square and his statues were removed. Prominent streets were renamed after revolutionary leaders such as Julius Nyerere and Samora Machel.

Another significant step towards national unity and political stability was the merging of the two rival parties into a single party under ZANU-PF in December 1987. A Unity

Accord was signed by the two leaders on 27 December 1987. An amnesty was granted to all dissidents, including members of the security forces. This move worried many as it was seen as a move to a one-party state, concentration of power in the hands of Mugabe and ultimately an end to democracy and the freedoms that people normally take for granted.

I was pleased that my contribution to the national liberation war was recognised by ZANU-PF. Once the country secured its independence, I was granted my own parcel of land in recognition of my contribution to the liberation struggle. Apart from gifts of land, other participants received gifts of money. In 1997, registered ex-combatants were paid Z$50,000 as a reward for service. The same amount was paid to male and female fighters. Around the same time, Prime Minister Mugabe began the process of nationalising land previously under the control of white Zimbabweans. The honeymoon with the whites had long ended. In 2001, the government introduced the Fast Track Land Reform Programme, also commonly referred to as the Third Chimurenga. This led to many white farmers fleeing the country with calamitous effects for the economy.

We have an expression in our Shona culture which says, *Shiri Yakangwara Inovaka Dendere Neminhenga Yedzimwe Shiri.* The equivalent translation of this saying is the old English adage which says, 'A successful woman is one who can build a firm foundation with the bricks others have thrown at her.' When I look back at my experiences, I have come to realise the truth of this saying. I was 13 years old when the war ended. I felt a sense of relief. The war had disrupted my childhood years. I had missed out on my education and the normal activities children take for granted such as playing with friends and living without fear. I returned to school and completed my education. When I finished school, I did not lose any time in getting married to my childhood boyfriend, *Last Gakanje*. We were brought up in the same district and went to the same primary school. We first met when I fell and hurt myself while I was taking part in a bottle race at school. He came to my aid when I fell. His kindness touched my heart. Some years later when he proposed to me, I did not hesitate to welcome him into my life.

When I was 18, I gave birth to our first child, Kudzai Phoebe who was born on 25 May 1985. This is a significant day in our calendar as this is when we celebrate *African Union Day* – formerly known as African Liberation Day. This day is a recognition of the liberation of Africa from colonial rule. Next to arrive in 1987 was another daughter Rangarirai Privilege, followed by three sons, Tatenda, Tagumanashe Joseph, and Takudzwa Victor, who was born in 1999. All of our children were educated in private schools and were never short of anything. They were taught English in schools run by white people. Today all five children have excelled in their chosen field. My older daughter is an electrical engineer. The second daughter is a successful lawyer and magistrate for the Victoria Falls Region. One of my sons is an environmental scientist. Another is a human resources manager and the youngest studied hospitality management. The youngest, Takudzwa Victor, was reunited with me in the UK in December 2018 and is now preparing to go to University.

Alongside bringing up my children, I also trained to be a dressmaker and a fashion designer. In 1987, I went to college in the province of Bulawayo in the Matabeleland region, to study fashion design. I completed my Diploma in 1989. I went on to establish my first business the following year in the affluent and thriving Hwange district, near Victoria Falls. The company was named Simangaliso Designers and the Shona equivalent is Zvishamiso which literally means 'Amazing Work'. The business was supported by a generous interest-free loan from the then Ministry of Gender and National Affairs. The money was to be repaid over 5 years. This business marked the beginning of my struggle for my gender empowerment.

My company's mission was to supply a wide range of indigenous textile products to schools, department stores and to the tourist and hospitality sectors that include hotels around the Victoria Falls and safaris such as Sinamatela Lodge. This area is the commercial centre of Zimbabwe and is very popular with tourists. Victoria Falls is one of the Seven Wonders of the World. The Scottish missionary and explorer, David Livingstone, is believed to have been the first European to set eyes on Victoria Falls on 16 November 1855. He recorded this as his discovery of the Victoria Falls in honour of Britain's Queen Victoria. The local Lozi language name is, Mosi-oa-Tunya or 'The Smoke That Thunders' (intutuziyathunqua), as it is widely known for its scenic view of mist caused by falling waters. Both names are recognised by the World Heritage Organisation.

Running this type of business in this busy part of Zimbabwe was a childhood ambition. I have always wanted to run my own business and become economically independent. From a young age, my passion was needlework. I was taught to sew by my mother and older sister Siluzile Marumisa who are both deceased. By the age of 10, I was repairing clothes for people in my village and sewing dresses for dolls. My business was very successful. I employed three full-time staff, including my accountant. During very busy periods, I also employed staff on a casual basis to do piece-rate work. This included supplying uniforms to schools. My products were rated very highly as a result, my order book was always full new contracts with many of the large hotels, game reserves, department stores and national parks in the country, including the famous Sinamatela Camp and Robins Camp. The company provided an interior design service to these businesses. I supplied them with bespoke curtains, bed linens, tablecloths, table runners and other textile products. We also provided repair services for damaged bedspreads, curtains and other textile wares. My sister, who worked in the fashion business in a large department store, sourced most of the business for my company. Many of these businesses were owned by white Rhodesians and foreign investors.

Although trading with these businesses was very

rewarding, it came with risks. Some segments of the population felt it was a sell-out to do business with those who had colonised and exploited our people. Others were more tolerant and accepted that the country needed the expertise and resources of everyone to build a vibrant economy.

Another strand of my company's operations was to support the then Ministry of Gender and National Affairs in the delivery of services to women who aspired to own and run their businesses. My business was used as a model to guide them on how they could translate their business vision into reality. My remit was to empower women to develop their skills and become self-sufficient. I was keen to demonstrate to them from my own example that it was possible to be a wife and mother, and run a successful business at the same time. I worked with both urban and rural communities, initiating business projects around sewing, flower arrangement, catering, poultry, livestock, transportation and other micro-enterprise ventures. I provided training, advice, mentoring, employment and enterprise support to the women. This included how to develop a business plan, set prices, manage resources, and monitor and evaluate the performance of their business. I did a lot of liaison work between communities and non-governmental organisations that funded most of our projects. These included the Red Cross and Food Aid Organisation. I encouraged the women to follow their passion and work hard. I wanted to see greater equality between women and men. This was a great motivating force for me. My vision was to see a marked and sustained improvement in the general welfare of everyone within my country. The liberation struggle would be a failure if all it did was to end white domination and replace this with another type of inequality spearheaded by indigenous Zimbabweans over their own people. I saw a great deal of progress in the living conditions of the rural and urban poor during the period after independence.

While these improvements were welcomed by some segments of the population, others wanted to see a faster pace of economic and social development. The political environment remained volatile. Mistrust between the Shona people and Ndebele tribe was rife. There was a widespread fear that dissidents were plotting with members of the deposed Rhodesian regime, aided and supported by Apartheid South Africa, to overthrow the Mugabe government. It was alleged that PF-ZAPU were also behind this plot. This led to Comrade Joshua Mqabuko Nyongolo Nkomo's dismissal from the government in 1982.

Anti-government protests followed and thousands of mainly Ndebele civilians lost their lives. Comrade Joshua Mqabuko Nyongolo Nkomo sought refuge in London before returning to take part in the 1985 elections. The civil unrest abated when the two parties signed a unity accord in December 1987 and became a single party under ZANU-PF. The Unity Accord pledged *'to unite our nation; establish peace, law and order and to guarantee social and economic development; ...to eliminate and end the insecurity and*

*violence caused by dissidents in Matabeleland.' It further states
'... that national unity, political stability and order, social and
economic development can only be achieved to their fullest
under conditions of peace and unity primarily of ZANU-PF
and PF-ZAPU.'*

Life for my family was relatively good. My husband was
a chief risk officer for ZESA company in Zimbabwe. He had
previously studied risk management in England. We owned
a huge house in the Victoria Falls area. Each of our children
had their own bedroom. There were also extra rooms for
guests. We employed two workers to help us with domestic
work, one of whom lived with us. In addition, I had help
from my extended family to look after the children while I
ran the business. Both my mother and my mother-in-law
would visit on a regular basis, usually for up to three months
at a time. My sisters went to school nearby and often stayed
with us. My brothers' children also visited us frequently. The
house was always full of people. I cannot remember carrying
the children on my back at any time.

My business was very successful. I took home far more
money at the end of each month than my husband. During
the post-independence period, many people still didn't
welcome the presence of whites. I was often criticised and
harassed for my business relationship with them. There was
a process to evict the white farmers. My trading with white
farmers was viewed as openly supporting them and endorsing
their former policies. I enjoyed my work but I began to get
nervous when security and government personnel started

to disrupt my trading activities. By 2000, this escalated to threats on my life. I received a number of threatening letters and verbal assaults. On one occasion, I was robbed of a large sum of money. Although these incidents were reported to the police, they were never recorded and investigated. I lived in growing fear. It was common for people to go missing and to be killed without any explanation. The practice of failing to investigate reported crimes was not unusual. The security forces had limited resources and, of necessity, chose to concentrate on what they regarded to be the most serious crimes. Although I was a young girl fighter Chimbwido who had campaigned for the liberation of my country, I ceased my militant activities once independence was secured. I did not criticise the government of the day. This did not mean that I was happy with all the government's domestic and foreign policies. I kept a low profile and focused on my work and family life. I did not want to be seen as an enemy of the state. The political environment remained tense and the civil unrest continued even after the two parties merged as a single party under ZANU-PF in December 1987.

There were further factors that compounded my sense of insecurity as I conducted my business on a day-to-day basis. I also found myself experiencing growing unrest at home. In a male-dominated society with gender inequalities, married life presented a host of challenges for a newly married woman. It didn't matter whether you were a woman working in a leadership position or a stay-at-home woman. As a woman, you were expected to see your primary role as a wife, child-bearer and caretaker for the home and your family. The family for us meant the extended family. In spite of legislative changes to address gender inequalities, the woman is still expected to show subservience to her husband and the members of his family. I did not have any problems with our culture and traditions. The problem was not with my relationship with my husband or my children or what they expected from me. It came from the cultural norms and traditions as they applied to the relationship between a daughter-in-law and a mother-in-law.

I was expected to move from my home to live in my mother-in-law's household. I was seen as an appendage to her family and I was expected to be at the service of all her family members. This was seen as a sign of being a good wife. In the mornings, I was expected to kneel down and say 'good morning mum' to my mother-in-law. I was expected to refer to the women in the family as aunties *vana tete* and to the men as uncles *vana baba mukuru* or *baba munini* or brother-in-law *varunyana* or *varume nyana*. The major part of my role was to meet their needs. If you were not accustomed to the culture, you would feel as though you were married to the whole family. I did not always feel very happy in the marriage as I sometimes felt the marriage was crowded. My husband and I wanted more time and space to devote to each other. There were times when my own needs didn't appear to count. It was my job to do the cooking, cleaning, washing, ironing and other household jobs. It did not matter that I was an independent and financially secure businesswoman. I did not have the right to name my own children. The cultural practices gave my mother-in-law a great deal of influence over household decisions, including how our money should be used and managed. It is common for women to face destitution following the death of their husbands, as their in-laws typically grab the property and all valuables from the widows. This practice is widely documented in the media and academic circles.

A report by Human Watch documents the scale of the abuse. The report states: *'No fewer than two thirds of the women who spoke to Human Rights Watch said they experienced the profound injustice of their in-laws taking over their homes or property, and feeling helpless to stop it. Others simply did not know that they had property and inheritance rights to begin with and were unable to withstand the intimidation tactics used by their in-laws such as daily shaming, harassment, and physical assaults. Others said that they were wary of jeopardising relationships with in-laws with whom they had shared their lives for many years, and whom they had hoped would support them and their children in familial and cultural ways.'* (*You Will Get Nothing – Violations of Property and Inheritance Rights of Widows in Zimbabwe, January 2017*).

The problem was dramatized in the blockbuster film, Neria (1993). *Neria* tells the story of a widowed woman whose brother-in-law tried to dispossess her of her home, all her other assets and even her children by abusing the traditional customs. This situation reminds me of a Shona proverb that says *chakupa ronda chati nhunzi dzikudye*. This is an old saying that my mother would use when there was an issue of concern. It means 'whatever has caused a wound to your body has exposed you to flies that will hurt you further'. The situation will demand you to have courage and be strong (kutoshinga).

When a woman's husband dies in Zimbabwe, she is left at the mercy of her in-laws. In some cases, the in-laws will ensure the widow's needs are always met. However, all too often, greed takes over and the widow finds herself deprived of a home and every material possession, and even her children. The problem is worse if the couple did not make a will and if the woman previously allowed her husband to manage their financial affairs. Under these circumstances, the in-laws usually dispossess the widow. If she tries to claim the estate, she will experience a lot of resistance, intimidation, insults and even physical assaults. Widows are unfairly labelled witches, prostitutes and good-for-nothing. They are blamed for the death of their husbands. This problem manifested itself when my husband died in 2013.

It is a problem that affects most Zimbabwean women in general. It cuts across class, tribe and rural-urban divide. Even when women try to seek redress through the Court system, it is often difficult to obtain justice. They face barriers such as lack of understanding about legal procedures, lack of access to free government support, lack of resources to pay legal fees, difficulties representing themselves in Court or lack of money to hire lawyers to assist them, and difficulties in providing documents to prove ownership of the disputed assets. The problem is further compounded by the type of marriage the woman had. A woman may find herself in one of three types of marriage in Zimbabwe: a civil marriage which is registered and where the man is only married to one woman; the customary law marriage which is also registered but where the man may have more than one wife; and the unregistered customary marriage. The latter two types of marriages often lack official documents to validate them. In cases of disputes, the Courts have to rely on evidence and confirmation from the in-laws to ascertain if the woman was married to the deceased husband. This is fraught with difficulties as the in-laws have vested interests in the deceased's property and will usually try to deny the existence of a marriage.

As I reflect, I realise that although I was an equal contributor to everything that was left in my late husband's estate, I was also faced with many of the issues which the novelist Tsitsi Dangarembwa wrote about and which were narrated in the film, *Neria*. My absence from home when he died made my situation more difficult. I was not there to claim what rightfully belonged to me. I was unfairly blamed for abandoning him when I fled to the UK. A number of my in-laws labelled me as a bad wife and a wicked woman. They attached all kinds of insulting labels on me, many of which are too vulgar to mention here.

I was married for 28 years and I was a very successful entrepreneur. Yet my in-laws claimed I contributed nothing to the marriage and the assets he left behind. I was expected to start all over again with nothing. They even attempted to strip me of my husband's surname – Gakanje.

'The Lady in Black'
(as a widow I was left alone with nothing)

A major challenge for me and other women who find themselves as widows is to fight against the customary laws which discriminate against women. Women should be entitled to inherit land and property on an equal basis with men. Government legislations and policies should give pride of place to women's empowerment, equality of opportunities and justice for all. The laws need to be modernised and fit for purpose. It is not sufficient to rely on customary law for the male in-laws to protect and provide for the woman once her husband has died. Women are capable of providing for themselves. The only protection women need is strong laws that recognise their rights and make discrimination a shameful thing of the past. This fight for gender equality and real empowerment for vulnerable women across Africa and other continents is a central plank of my organisation's work programme. Our experience can shape and inform our life purpose.

I believe God has put me through these harsh experiences so that I can help other people who find themselves in a similar position to what I endured. I was an independent woman with my own business, not a stay-at-home wife who was dependent on my husband's resources. My business venture was very profitable and I was generous with the money I earned. My husband was free to use his money as he wished. I did not discourage him from giving financial support to his relatives. I knew before our marriage that my mother-in-law had lost her husband and that my husband was her main breadwinner. He was the second of four sons but the other two sons did not have the financial means to provide for her. Her other sons did not have a well-paid job. I was always willing to give money and other gifts to the members of my husband's family. Notwithstanding this kindness, we did not always live in peace and harmony. My mother-in law acted as though I was in competition with her or a threat to her livelihood. Nothing could be further from the truth. Despite the fact that I would give her money and other gifts on top of what my husband would regularly give to her, she was hard to please. She did not want me to own anything. I tried hard to live in peace with her and the other members of her family but this was impossible. They always frustrated me and had a way of making my life miserable. The problems I experienced went beyond the cultural norms. It is well-known and accepted in our culture that a mother-in-law is an important figure and should be loved and respected. I accepted this as a cultural given. However, there were times when I felt like an intruder. Basically there was no respect from the family, who would treat me like a stranger. As a senior daughter-in-law I was never involved in the family discussions and that made me an angry, bitter woman in the circles of vultures.

The tensions in our household put a huge strain on my marriage and family life. I felt squashed and stifled. It could easily have caused our marriage to break-down but neither of us wanted a divorce. We were inseparable. My husband and I tried to spend as much time as possible together with our children. We were both working in the city but we were expected to return to her home on weekends and when we were on holidays. The other members of her family treated me with the same contempt. They insulted me and made false allegations. They accused me of being a prostitute who went for the war veterans and white businessmen. My business relationships with male business owners were sometimes misconstrued. I was expected to be available whenever any member of the family needed my services, even if it was not convenient for me.

My husband hated to see me in distress. He tried in vain to create a happy and harmonious environment for all of us. I found myself unhappy in my private life at home and unhappy at work due to the mounting harassment from security and other personnel because of my business links with white people. I experienced violence from all sides. It felt like a double source of injustice and disempowerment. This was what drove me to devise a plan to flee the country. Although I consider myself to be resilient, I could not bear any more. I wanted to be free to pursue my dreams and to feel fully empowered. The plan had the full support of my husband and my children – those who were old enough to understand.

In 2002, when I decided to leave Zimbabwe, my youngest child was just two years.

There were many socio-economic problems which remained largely intact from the era of white minority. These included poverty, mass unemployment, hyperinflation, poor housing, poor health and uneven distribution of wealth and income. The economy of Zimbabwe shrank significantly after 2000. This was in sharp contrast to the growth recorded in the economy in the first three years after independence when foreign aid and new investment poured into the country. Expertise and other resources were lost when farms and land were seized from white farmers. This led to a sharp fall in export crops such as cotton, tobacco, tea, coffee, maize, peanuts and fruits.

The situation deteriorated further as a result of

Zimbabwe's participation from 1998 to 2002 in the civil war in the Democratic Republic of the Congo. Sanctions imposed by Britain, the United States and other western governments also took its toll on the economy. Martin Meredith describes the state of the Zimbabwean economy by the end of the 1990s as follows:

'By the end of the 1990s Zimbabwe was in dire straits. The unemployment rate had risen to more than 50 per cent. Only one-tenth of the number of pupils leaving school was able to find formal employment. Inflation had reached 60 per cent. The value of wages in real terms had fallen over ten years by 22 per cent. On average, the population of 13 million was 10 per cent poorer at the end of the 1990s than at the beginning. More than 70 per cent lived in abject poverty. Hospitals were short of drugs and equipment; government schools were starved of funds; state organisations were bankrupt; the public transport system was decrepit; fuel supplies were erratic; scores of businesses had closed. Harare, once renowned as one of the cleanest cities in Africa, was noted now for debris on the pavements, cracked cement paving, broken street lights, potholes, uncollected refuse and burst pipelines. Martin Meredith, *The Fate of Africa* (2005, p.636).'

Notwithstanding the disastrous state of the economy, my decision to seek asylum was not influenced in any way by economic factors. I was financially secure and my business was doing well in spite of the economic decline. The decisive factors were domestic and political. It was purely about taking steps to preserve my life and ultimately to be alive for my children. The decision to flee and leave everything I owned behind was a necessity – not a light decision borne out of perceived material gains.

CHAPTER FOUR

NAVIGATING THE MAZE OF THE UK ASYLUM SYSTEM

'Everyone has the right to seek and to enjoy in other countries asylum from persecution'
  Article 14 (1) The Universal Declaration of Human Rights

This chapter discusses my hopes and expectations when I took the bold step to flee my country. It contrasts this with the grim reality I encountered in the United Kingdom and my long and protracted battle with the asylum system.

MY ARRIVAL IN THE UNITED KINGDOM

There is an expression which says time flies. This feels true for me when I look back. I remember vividly Wednesday 17 July 2002 when I landed at Gatwick Airport. I arrived in the United Kingdom on a six-month visitor's visa and it was a cold day although it was in the peak of summer. I did not know that my experiences with the asylum system would be as harsh as the weather that greeted me on arrival. My expectations in coming to the United Kingdom were to live in an environment where law and order are observed. I wanted to be able to express my views on current affairs without fear of persecution. As an ambitious and highly skilled woman, I also wanted the freedom to work and be economically independent so that I could help to look after my family. I did not come expecting to live on state handouts. All I wanted was a safe haven where I could resume my entrepreneurial activities and provide, not just for myself, but also generate employment and other benefits for my host country. I thought I would be welcome here as Zimbabwe has strong historical and economic ties with the UK.

Apart from the inhospitable weather, my first day did not work out as I had expected. I was taken aback by the fact that everyone seemed so serious. Immigration officers came across as serious and business-minded if not sad, unhappy and unwelcoming. I didn't expect the customs officers to rummage through my suitcase and other luggage. They combed through every item in my luggage, including my undergarments. In my culture, it is forbidden for a man to handle a lady's personal effects. As this was my first long-distance flight, I did not know that it was against the law to travel with sharp items. As my sewing accessories have always been a part of me, they were among the first items I packed in my suitcase. Ever since I mastered the skill of sewing, I never went anywhere without my tape measure, scissors and needles. I felt badly hurt when the customs officers confiscated my scissors and needles. I implored in vain for them to allow me to take the items with me.

After what seemed like hours, I finally emerged through the formalities of the customs process and made my way to the reception area, where I was expecting to be met by someone. As the plane had arrived late and I was further delayed going through the immigration and customs process, the person who had come to meet me had decided to leave. I now found myself alone, surrounded by foreigners, some 5,148 miles away from home. I thought about my family, my friends and everything I had left behind in my beloved country and wondered how my husband and children were coping without me. We were a very close and supportive family which functioned as a team. Every member of our family, including the youngest child, had a distinct role to play. As a very successful textile designer, I shared the role of breadwinner with my husband. At the same time, I took my domestic and housekeeping duties seriously. I enjoyed preparing delicious food for my family, making clothes for my family and keeping my home clean and tidy.

Although I found myself immersed in nostalgia, it was not long before I was forced to face my new reality and the challenges that lay ahead. My first challenge was to find my way to London, where I stayed for my first six weeks with a former church colleague whom I had known in Zimbabwe. Unlike many new arrivals to the UK, I did not have to worry about currency conversion. In my textiles business in Zimbabwe, I was frequently paid in pounds sterling and had amassed enough for my journey to the UK.

My first impressions of the people were not wholly positive. Their body language was closed and unwelcoming. I needed help with directions but I did not feel I could ask a question. Before I left Zimbabwe I had been told not to ask anyone other than the police for directions as some people take pleasure in misdirecting unwelcome foreigners to their shores. On the train, I noticed people had their heads buried in newspapers or books. Everyone seemed to be in a world of their own as they kept close guard over their personal space. I scanned the carriage carefully to find a suitable seat where I could sit. I felt uncomfortable. The lady I sat next to did not even raise her head to look at me. Like every other person in that carriage, she was glued to her newspaper until the train arrived in London.

I was overwhelmed when I alighted in London. I saw tall buildings, a network of narrow roads and rail lines, heavy traffic, fast moving people who appeared to mind their own business. Buildings were either terraced or close to each other. It took me a while to understand why they were situated so close to each other and 'joined-up' in straight lines with very little open space. I was accustomed to living in what Zimbabweans call low-density accommodation surrounded by vast tracts of land with orchards and forest land. I was surprised that very few houses had vacant land for the children to play ball games without having to go to the communal park. I missed the site of African houses with their mosaic of simple materials like thatch, mud bricks, stones, poles and wood. What confused me even more were the sirens of ambulances, fire-engines and police vehicles. These sirens startled me to a point where I became emotionally disturbed.

After six weeks in London, I moved to Nottingham, where the cost of living is lower than in London and I was likely to meet other people from Zimbabwe. Arrangements were made for someone to meet me and provide me with accommodation but again I was let down. For the first time in my life, I found myself homeless and alone, living precariously. After a number of weeks, a very kind Jamaican lady offered me temporary accommodation until the Home Office provided me with accommodation.

My decision to come to the UK was truly life-changing. It was hard to leave my family behind in Zimbabwe. It was just as hard for them to see me leave but they too had real fears about my safety. My main expectation was to find a safe environment where I could live and work. My vision was to set up a business and carry on from where I had left off in Zimbabwe. I wanted to make a positive contribution to society. Contrary to the popular narrative, I had no wish to rely on government handouts or benefits. I was brought up in a proud and affluent family where we were taught from a very young age to be independent and self-sufficient. My journey to the United Kingdom was challenging because I was running away from my own country, seeking protection from persecution by the secret agencies of the government in Zimbabwe, where I was persecuted for dealing with whites. During the aftermath of independence in Zimbabwe, my position as a business woman trading with white farmers and business owners placed me on a collision course with the authorities at a time when government policy was to confiscate their property and expel them from the country. As a result, I faced systematic persecution from members of my husband's family who maliciously accused me of having an illicit relationship with war veterans. When I arrived in the United Kingdom, I did not think that I was breaking the law in any way. In my mind, I was simply exercising my human rights to seek protection in a signatory country of the 1951 Geneva Convention Relating to the Status of Refugees. I thought my rights would be upheld so long as I could demonstrate that I faced a well-founded fear of persecution on grounds of race, religion, nationality, political opinion or membership of a particular social group.

MY EXPERIENCE WITH THE ASYLUM PROCESS

Like many refugees from across the world who live in the United Kingdom today, I harboured the hope of returning to Zimbabwe within my first six months so long as the risk to my personal safety was removed. Unfortunately this did not happen. Even whilst I was out of the country, I continued to live in fear. On several occasions, I received threatening telephone calls from 'men in dark glasses', secret agencies. I felt as though I was constantly under surveillance. I did not feel free to move about as I wished. I also found it hard to trust people with my telephone number and other personal information. This forced me to apply to normalise my stay in the United Kingdom. I made an application for asylum in December 2002.

It took almost nine years for my asylum application to be processed and upheld. What a far cry from the rhetoric published in Home Office policy documents! The Home Office has widely publicised its target to make decisions on 98% of 'straightforward asylum claims' within six months. Readers should note the loaded wording used by the Home Office to define this service standard. By using the term 'straightforward asylum claims', they can easily fudge the statistics and disguise poor performance. Any claim which is not processed within six months can be simply dismissed as 'complex' and not 'straightforward'. The absence of a definition of a straightforward asylum claim makes it easy to disguise poor performance and injustice to asylum seekers. Interestingly, an investigation carried out by the chief inspector of borders and immigration found out that roughly 50 per cent of the asylum cases handled by the Home Office are being categorised as 'non-straightforward' in order to exclude them from the six-month decision target. The chief inspector reported that 'a significant number of these claims should never have been categorised as non-straightforward.'

There was nothing 'complex' about my case. I was a vulnerable woman facing the real risk of persecution. Upon reflection, I still cannot understand why it should have taken almost a whole decade to process and uphold my application. My application was rejected four times before it was finally upheld on the fifth attempt. Each time I turned up for an interview or hearing I encountered a different team with very little knowledge of my case. I found myself repeating myself, outlining the same story time and again.

I had a valid case but the authorities did not believe me. There were times when I was deprived of the help and support that I needed to help me to present my case effectively. Initially I was provided with legal support but this aid ceased after my second refusal. After this, I had to turn to the voluntary sector and private individuals for help with legal support. For my first interview I also had the support of an interpreter. After that they withdrew it as they claimed my level of English was 'adequate'. This was far from being the case. I still felt I needed this type of support as a lot of what was said in many of these interviews went over my head. It is true that English is one of the official languages in Zimbabwe. However, this does not mean every Zimbabwean has mastery of it. Fluency and competence in English largely depends on your level of education and age. In my case, my mother tongue is Shona. Those of us from my region who speak some form of English speak a variant of English blended with our own indigenous languages. My knowledge of the English language was basic and I did not feel well equipped to present my case. Sixteen years on, my English has improved considerably, after long periods of study at The People's College and Derby University. I took classes in English as I wanted to learn to present my case effectively.

The caseworkers at the Home Office failed to assess

my claim fairly and sympathetically. Sometimes it felt as though they had already made the decision about my claim before the actual hearing. I didn't feel respected or listened to. I recall on one occasion when I appeared before the tribunal panel on the day when the funeral for my father was taking place. I sobbed uncontrollably. The authorities misconstrued my tears and rejected my asylum claim. They thought I was crying to influence their decision. They finally suspended my legal aid. For that reason, from that time on I was classified as an illegal person.

The members of staff were not trained to understand our cultural practices. This invariably results in unfair decisions. The experience of going to court or to a meeting to represent myself was alien to my culture. Up until recently, women were not allowed to represent themselves in my culture. This was done for them by their husbands or a male figure with social standing. If my mum had a problem with a neighbour and this resulted in court action or an official complaint to the authorities, it would be my father's responsibility to deal with the issue on her behalf, hence the expression *kurova mukadzi wemunhu isimba kaviri*. This literally means 'if you bit someone's wife you should be prepared for a big fight with the husband'. Girls were not allowed in the 1970s to go to school. Women's rights were often abused. They had difficulties getting identification cards, obtaining credit and well paid jobs. As a chief, my father broke the norm and empowered my sisters and me. We were given the opportunity to obtain an education.

The British government did not accommodate different cultural norms. In my culture, when we speak to people in authority, we do not look at them in the face as a sign of respect. This is different from the UK norm where you are expected to look into people's eyes during conversations or interviews. Sometimes I lost my appeals because I did not look the interviewer in the eye. The Home Office staff interpreted my tendency to look down or away from them during my interviews as a sign that I was providing them with false information.

Each time my case was rejected my life became harder. Once my status changed to 'failed asylum seeker', I lost entitlement to money to support me and to all other forms of support – including housing. I was expected to return home voluntarily or face forcible deportation after my second failed asylum claim. Once my benefits were withdrawn, I lived in abject poverty. As an asylum seeker, I had previously received a weekly allowance of £37.75 while my claim was being considered. I was also provided with housing. The allowance was paid in vouchers which could only be redeemed in designated outlets.

It works out at a little over £5 per day. It was an insult to live on this paltry sum. I could not afford to buy my traditional food. As far as possible, I had to content myself with potatoes and other food which was not always welcome to my palate. Although African food is widely available in Nottingham, this is very expensive compared to locally produced food. I had to walk everywhere and rely on food aid and clothing banks to meet much of my basic needs. The food from the food banks was not always suitable. It was used food, which in most cases had passed the expiry or 'best before' date. I know someone who nearly died from food poisoning after she had eaten food from a corroded can that had passed its 'use by' date.

Perhaps the most serious problem from being a 'failed asylum seeker' was the loss of accommodation. My support from the National Asylum Service ended the moment my asylum claim was rejected. My landlord could no longer accommodate me and I was automatically forced into the street. I was made homeless seven times. The first time this happened to me, I did not know what to do or who to turn to for help as I hardly knew anyone in the United Kingdom. I was picked up by a certain elderly lady when I was roaming the street in desperation for accommodation. This woman who was riding a scooter stopped and asked me why I was crying. I told her I felt lost and helpless. She was moved to tears when she learned I was thrown out of my accommodation. She offered me temporary shelter at her home.

On another occasion when I became homeless, I took up shelter for six months in a dilapidated building in Station Street, Nottingham, where the old police station was based before it moved to North Sherwood Street. The building was infested with rats and cockroaches. It had no running water, no heating and no furniture. I didn't even have a bed. Whenever the opportunity arose, I would take a bath or shower in other people's homes. More often than not, I had to settle for 'a top and tail' in a bucket with water. In spite of the poor condition of the building, it has a special meaning to me. My umbilical cord was buried there. The ideas for many of the social projects which I subsequently launched came to me while I was living in this substandard building. With the help of a good friend, Dianne Skerritt, I spent many sleepless nights working on my business plan and writing bids. This was the early beginning of Nottingham African Women's Empowerment Forum (NAWEF).

One of the problems of homelessness and frequent address changes is abuse of your personal data. If important letters with your personal details end up in the wrong hands, this can result in identity theft and other fraudulent activities. Although no one wants to take on the identity of an asylum seeker, this does not stop criminals from using your information to obtain credit. This was exactly what happened to me. Someone used my data to buy £1,200 worth of goods in Littlewoods. I faced immense difficulties to prove my innocence. After a lengthy investigation, my name was finally cleared. I attribute problems like this to the policies of the Home Office. Frequent re-housing of asylum seekers and withdrawal of their accommodation creates the conditions for a breach of asylum claimants' data rights. The Home Office owe asylum seekers and refugees a duty of care to handle their personal information in line with the provisions of the Data Protection Act. I know many asylum seekers and refugees who have had similar experiences to mine. Many have missed Home Office appointments, as letters about meetings have got lost or sent to the wrong address. They do not seem to have proper systems to track claimants' up-to-date addresses.

The Home Office needs to recognise that asylum-seekers with failed applications have the same needs as those whose applications are under consideration. They also have a need for food, clothing, shelter, healthcare and other services to meet their basic needs. There needs to be equality of service. The person is a human-being with rights to fundamental services regardless of their status. Everyone should be given access to these basic services regardless of the outcome of their asylum application. It is this failure which has led some failed asylum-seekers to abscond, work in the so-called 'black-economy' and engage in illegal activities.

It was difficult to comprehend why the government would treat asylum-seekers in such an inhumane way. I have come to understand from public commentaries that keeping people in destitution is a key strand of the government's policy to force asylum-seekers to leave the country and to discourage others from seeking asylum in the United Kingdom. Rt Hon Iain Duncan Smith MP Preface to *Restoring Trust in the UK Asylum System*, The Centre for Social Justice: Asylum and Destitution Working Group, December 2008 argues that 'It also appears that the British government is using forced destitution as a means of encouraging people to leave voluntarily.' In the report, Dr Chris McDowell further observes: 'The asylum system has developed into a process that is more about controlling numbers than deciding who needs protection.[5]' The reader should note that the government's policy of hostility takes a number of different forms. Among other things, this is reflected in its 'dispersal strategy' whereby asylum seekers are not given a voice in where they live or the paltry amount of money allocated for their subsistence; in the inept approach to processing asylum applications; in exclusion from labour market participation; in social isolation; in the frequent reporting regime at regional reporting centres; and in the propensity to detain certain categories of asylum seekers.

Detaining asylum seekers for long periods is another strategy which was being used by Home Office. While I was fortunate enough to avoid detention, I have some experience of visiting other brothers and sisters who have been placed for long periods in detention centres; as part of my NAWEF remit, I have actively supported women who were in and out of detention centres. I was instrumental in championing the cause of asylum seekers even though at the time I had not yet gained refugee status.

It has now become clear that Home Office staff are driven by meeting targets – ticking boxes rather than listening properly to asylum-seekers' stories and seeking to make the right decision. This was confirmed by a former caseworker in an anonymous public letter to The *Guardian* (8 April 2017)[6] quoting an anonymous Home Office caseworker who said, 'I worry asylum caseworkers are failing people in their darkest hour ... At the Home Office we're moulded to be sceptical and work to unrealistic targets. Doing the right thing can mean taking a performance hit.'

In a more recent disclosure to journalists from *The Guardian*, three former Home Office caseworkers shed further light on the problems inherent in the asylum process. They described the asylum process as a 'lottery'. We are told that asylum interviews are 'rushed', 'biased', 'intimidatory' and the outcome often takes the form of 'cut and paste' decisions from previous cases. The starting position is that asylum seekers are 'liars'. As one whistle-blower put it: 'an attitude of cynicism towards asylum seekers became "a part of you"' (*The Guardian*, 11 February 2018)[7].

This perception influences the way Home Office staff approach their work. Some caseworkers apparently take pleasure in rejecting application claims without weighing up the evidence to judge the merit of the claim. Decisions are not always objective. It sometimes boils down to which caseworker was allocated to your case and their mood at a given point in time. Someone remarked that the way the Home Office handles cases of asylum seekers is like a lottery because if you've got a caseworker who is particularly refusal-minded and is determined to catch you out then you're going to have a hard time. Inside information revealed that there are some enthusiasts who have a reputation for never granting anything who seem to take pride in that. Significantly, the whistle-blowers also drew attention to issues relating to poor training for their roles, overwork and the drawbacks of a target-driven culture. Staff are set an annual target of processing 225 claims or decision reports, which many find to be unrealistic. One whistle-blower described the challenge as follows: 'It affects the quality of the decisions … By the time you have been through the photos, the file, the news reports, it's three o'clock and then you have to draft a report, a decision on someone's claim, which can often be more than 20 pages long, which is difficult to complete in two hours. Another whistle-blower complained about lack of time to prepare for interviews. They shared with reporters that sometimes one does not get the file before the interview, so one does not know what the case is about. As a result you really start from scratch. You're asking really open-ended questions like: *'Can you tell me why you left X?'* This tends to embarrass the case workers.

The whistle-blowers' disclosure brought back echoes of former Home Secretary, John Reid's remarks in 2006 that the Home Office was 'not fit for purpose'. He told members of the Home Affairs Select Committee: 'Our system is not fit for purpose. It is inadequate in terms of its scope; it is inadequate in terms of its information technology, leadership, management systems and processes.'

Following this damning assessment, the Department was restructured and a more streamlined asylum process was introduced in March 2007 known as the New Asylum Model. At the time when the New Asylum Model was introduced, there was a huge backlog of cases. This was estimated at up to 450,000. A target was set by the Home Secretary for this to be cleared within 5 years. Willman and Knafler (*Support for asylum-seekers and other migrants : a guide to legal and welfare rights.* London, Legal Action Group, 2009) note that, 'Part of the backlog was cleared by UKBA issuing legacy questionnaires to individuals, many of whom had been waiting for an initial decision for more than three years.'

Significantly, I noticed a change in the culture after these changes were introduced. I began to see a glimpse of light at the end of the tunnel. There was a welcome improvement in the way my case was handled. I saw greater continuity in the personnel who were tasked with processing my application. Far greater effort was now made to listen to interviewees. The interviews felt less threatening. For the first time, I felt as though they were ready to genuinely understand my case and what would happen to me if I was forcibly deported back to Zimbabwe.

THE BIG BREAKTHROUGH

I was finally granted leave to remain in 2010. I remember the day when the letter arrived. Although I was looking forward to receiving the letter, I felt very apprehensive about opening it. I didn't want to raise my hopes and have them dashed yet again. Shaking like a plant on a very windy day, I finally summoned up the courage to open the letter. I was so happy that I burst into tears. Once the news began to sink in, I made a number of calls to share it with members of my family and the people who had helped me and kept me going during my struggle.

Although I had to wait for almost nine years, I was

pleased that my case for asylum was finally upheld. People sometimes asked me what, if anything, I could have done differently to help the authorities to handle my case more effectively. This is a difficult question to answer since I had no control over how the Home Office staff went about doing their work. One clear lesson that I learned is that it is important to give strong evidence to support your case, and to structure the information clearly and concisely. I did not want to jump all over the place and muddle the evidence. There is an English saying that 'ignorance is no defence'. If you don't know how to structure your case, the system does not make any allowance for this even when it is clear you have a valid case. With hindsight, I realise that it is also important to present your case confidently and maintain eye contact with the interviewers, even if this means departing from your cultural norms. I also realise that the evidence should go beyond the standard information such as the reason why you are seeking protection and the political and human rights situation in your home country. The evidence should include your conduct and what you have contributed to the UK since your arrival. It is also helpful to include written evidence from UK-based personnel who can comment independently on your character and how you have conducted yourself in your community.

Every asylum case is unique. However, I was pleased that my Indefinite Leave to Remain letter acknowledged my huge contribution to the voluntary sector since my arrival in the UK. Although I did not have the right to undertake paid employment, I channelled my skills and experience into volunteering. I am not the type of person to sit on my laurels and waste time. During my years of waiting in limbo, although this was psychologically damaging, I served as a volunteer worker in a large number of Nottingham-based organisations. In addition, I have been involved in a plethora of public campaigns addressing a range of issues which impact on asylum seekers and which were direct consequences of a failed asylum system. A notable example was 'Reunite Me with My Children'. It is important to note that all the organisations that volunteer asylum seekers involved themselves in had no clue about the plight of the asylum seekers. The organisations started editing most of their paperwork in line with what they were learning direct from asylum seekers. For me, too, it was a learning opportunity. I must confess that the experiences I got from interacting with both the organisers and asylum seekers helped me in a way to restructure my application papers. So when I look back to the success of my asylum claim, the single most important factor boiled down to how I structured and presented my case. Although Home Office staff rejected my application multiple times and demanded 'fresh evidence' each time, I did not have any new information to present. All I did was to submit the same evidence but in a more cogent and coherent manner.

I am grateful to all the people who helped me in my search for a safe environment where I can live my life and do what God created me to do. I owe the greatest debt of gratitude to my deceased father who brought me up to be strong and resilient. It was this quality of self-belief and resilience that kept me going during the difficult times. The biggest benefit of obtaining refugee status is stability and freedom. I am now able to make plans and make good use of my time.

CHAPTER FIVE

CULTURAL AND INTEGRATION CHALLENGES

This chapter discusses the challenges I experienced in accessing public services and integrating into the local community as an asylum seeker. These challenges were made worse by the government's 'hostile immigration environment policy' and the consequent lack of a meaningful integration strategy for asylum seekers and refugees with suitable orientation support.

'People seeking asylum arrive in the UK with almost nothing. Many have made a long and perilous journey. War and persecution have forced them to flee the homes they love. They hope and expect that they will receive a compassionate welcome. But for too many, the asylum system that they are confronted with in the United Kingdom is a hostile one, characterised by long delays, poor decisions, and a total lack of information.' (Refugee Action, *Waiting in the Dark, 2018*)[8].

The above quote is instructive in several ways. The second part of it quite rightly points out that the UK asylum system is far from welcoming and inclusive. The phrase 'But for too many, the asylum system that they are confronted with in the UK is a hostile one' sums up my experience very well. The government has deliberately designed a harsh asylum policy to discourage asylum seekers from coming to the United Kingdom. For this reason, very little attention is given to services to help asylum seekers to settle quickly and integrate into the local community. Yet all the evidence demonstrates that policies and services to support the integration of asylum seekers would benefit not just the asylum seekers, but also the host country.

One might wonder how a country like the United Kingdom, which preaches democracy and human rights, flouts the same human rights they talk about. The government's 'hostile environment' takes a number of forms. These include:

- the absence of a meaningful and supportive integration strategy;
- processing asylum applications slowly and unsympathetically;
- keeping asylum seekers in a state of limbo so that they cannot set and pursue meaningful goals;
- imposing a dispersal policy and refusing to give asylum seekers a say in where they are located;
- separating asylum seekers from others from a similar country or culture – including breaking up the family – and moving them frequently from one home to another

to make it difficult for them to settle and feel a sense of belonging;

- subjecting them to a draconian reporting regime where they have to report in person to the police station frequently, often travelling long distances;
- treating them with disrespect and indignity by giving vouchers instead of cash for their subsistence;
- keeping them financially destitute;
- putting them in detention for minor misdemeanours.

An inquiry into the treatment of asylum seekers by the Joint Committee on Human Rights found a wealth of evidence to confirm what the researchers term 'a deliberate policy of destitution'[9]. with the twin objectives of forcing failed asylum seekers to return to their home country and to deter other asylum seekers from coming to the UK. The Home Office has confirmed this policy and justifies it by stating that 'those not prioritised for removal... should be denied the benefits and privileges of life in the UK and experience an increasingly uncomfortable environment so that they elect to leave.'[10]

Whilst I agree with the second part of the quote at the top of this chapter about the lack of a compassionate welcome, I strongly object to the opening statement that 'People seeking asylum arrive in the UK with almost nothing.' Asylum seekers are a heterogeneous group. Each of them is unique with their own story for why they flee countries for safety. This is recognised in the legislations stating the grounds on which someone can claim asylum. It includes factors such as escape from war and other forms of indiscriminate violence; having a political opinion; attending a place of worship; belonging to a social group; and having an identity which is different from the mainstream population. For example, people may be persecuted on grounds of their sexual orientation, ethnicity, gender or physical appearance.

Whilst they may flee to the host country without material possessions, they bring with them a host of resources which their oppressors cannot take away from them. They bring with them their resilience, courage, strength, drive, creativity, skills, knowledge, qualifications, labour market experience and entrepreneurial flair. If they are made welcome and properly integrated into the host country, asylum seekers can be a huge asset as is so strikingly evident from the following examples:

- Without Joseph Malin, a Jewish refugee, there would probably be no fish and chips culture in the UK. He established the world's first fish and chip shop on Cleveland Street, London in 1860.
- Marks and Spencer owes its origins to Michael Marks, a Polish refugee;
- Alec Issigonis who designed the Mini motorcar, a global export, was a Turkish refugee who fled to the UK in 1906.

In my own case, I came with a wide range of skills,

qualifications, business experience and other personal qualities which remained largely untapped during my asylum ordeal. It is for this reason that I give the title *A Life Robbed* to my debut book. My life was taken away from me for almost a whole decade while I was kept waiting in limbo for the Home Office to make a suitable decision on my asylum application. During that time I could not make firm and meaningful plans to use my skills and experience to help disadvantaged groups. I lived in fear of forcible deportation. I found myself socially isolated, homeless and destitute. My mental and physical health suffered. I had to put the vision for my life and career on hold for years. I felt as though I was robbed of my power and my God-given gifts. Since gaining refugee status in 2010, I have moved on to establish an award-winning fashion business, FaGee Fashions Ltd. I have also helped thousands of asylum seekers, refugees, migrants, victims of domestic violence and other vulnerable people, through the work of the African Women's Employment Forum, which I founded while I was awaiting a decision from the Home Office on my asylum claim. If I had been allowed to use my gifts earlier, when I came to the UK, I would have been able to make a far greater contribution to the lives of disadvantaged people and to the wider UK society.

Giving confidence and support

The African Women's Empowerment Forum gives a voice to the vulnerable. For Refugee Week, **Erik Petersen** meets its inspirational founder

THE Home Office granted Faith Gakanje leave to remain in the UK this January, ending a seven-year ordeal. Faith Gakanje came to Britain from Zimbabwe.

She spent nearly a decade fighting the Government, giving to overcome the Government's refusal of her asylum claim. It gives us a bad that, she says.

But she has been welcomed in Gervok, she likely would have stayed in England. She did not have struggled for years with being an asylum seeker barred from work, moved from accommodation to accommodation to accommodation, of destination.

As without seeing those that took them from her life they had, she would not have decided to help others have. She is the same situation, what the African Women's Empowerment Forum. Its battle is on several fronts. It

Empowering: Pauline Edwards, arts coordinator at The African Women's Empowerment Forum, Celestine Bablo, activity coordinator and Ruth Heini, administrator, are pictured at City Arts with some of their sewing work.

how strong we are.

"The confidence they had... thanking legal system, little to no funds and no right to work. At the same time, they often come from highly patriarchal cultures that can make men strongly resist their own choices. In a refugee camp most women's group events. Currently, the group meets at City Arts, in Radford, and funding So the forum works to give

serves people who must face a women, confidence and support. To give them voice.

"Practically speaking, it or port. African clothes and pinafores everything from trying to arts to social and child care. From the group now, the proceeds will go towards helping destitute women who are asylum seekers.

The sewing project has been a major success for the forum,

trying to secure a nearby shop where they can sell some of the clothes and goods their women. From the

---

Faith
Gakanje

It's so sad
when you
fall into
poverty

Celestine Bablo, a founding member, runs it. She's from Congo, even she met Faith in 2008, when she spoke virtually no English.

"I stayed at home, I didn't go out because of English," Celestine said.

"Faith told me 'Celestine, your problem is not English'." With Celestine in the cause bringing her out to events, and gradually making her more confident.

It is a pattern the women involved with it found tend to tell similar stories. By chance they met Faith, or heard of Faith, and by the end of the conversation, Faith told them that they were needed.

Faith built an Eritrean and several other friends met Faith recently when they were all staying at the YMCA. Faith saw the women at the YMCA is a place that's not nice for a woman.

"People would advise she advised me. Who needed help, she helped me.

Now, Faith works for the forum and talks about going to university. She wants to work for the United Nations.

But if the group has succeeded, Faith's largely succeeded. Faith's remarks; it needs more to move on and expand.

The Home Office needs to do more to understand the needs of asylum seekers, their skills and experience, their goals and aspirations, and to help them to settle quickly and integrate into the community whilst their applications are being processed. It needs to develop an integration strategy with input from all stakeholder organisations, including contributions from asylum seekers and refugees. If such a strategy had been in place, my family and I would not have experienced the problems we went through. The problems I endured went beyond homelessness, social isolation, discrimination and economic destitution, for they also affected my physical and mental health, as the reader will see in the next chapter where I discuss this issue in more detail.

During my first contact with the Home Office, I was surprised that no one provided me with a 'Welcome Pack'. I have also discovered recently that migrants from EU countries have mandatory induction programmes for newly arrived asylum seekers, which other nationalities are deprived of. There are also structured policies for integrating EEA members into the country while their application is being processed. In the absence a similar resource available to me, I was obliged to rely on hearsay from other asylum seekers and refugees on what services were available and what lessons I could learn from their experience. I did not receive any information about my rights as an asylum seeker during the asylum process, and what entitlements to expect in the event my application were successful and refugee status was granted.

As I reflect on my asylum experience, I wish the Home Office had clarified from the outset how the asylum process works. I wish they had told me that there is no set timescale for how long the process takes. I was shocked that it took them almost a decade to decide on my application. The work which I currently do to support asylum seekers and refugees shows that the process can even take decades. I know someone who has been waiting for over 20 years for their asylum application to be processed. There is anecdotal evidence that there are asylum seekers who have been kept in a state of limbo for even longer. For example, information obtained by *The Guardian* newspaper under the Freedom of Information Act found that one person had to wait for as long as 26 years (*The Guardian*, 17 August 2018)[11]. While people are waiting for their asylum claim to be processed, they are not allowed to work. In my view, this is inhumane. As the Chief Executive of Refugee Action, Stephen Hale, comments: *'Forcing some people to wait more than 15 years for a decision on their asylum claim while banned from work and living below the poverty line is utterly barbaric'* (*The Guardian*, 17 August 2018)[12].

Policymakers also need to give careful consideration to the housing of asylum seekers and their welfare needs whilst they are waiting for their application to be processed. They should aim to keep families together and keep people from similar cultures together so that they can help each other. This would help them to settle down more easily, reduce anxiety and promote their general well-being. The policy of isolating people from their culture, friends and natural social networks is deplorable. Asylum seekers should be given a say in the decisions about where they can live and who they share accommodation with. The vast majority are randomly assigned to properties in the poorest parts of the country where housing is comparatively cheap. In the words of one anonymous female asylum seeker, *'Usually the G4S people (one of the government's providers), they give you accommodation where no one else wants to live and life is very difficult – crime is very high, there's prostitution, addiction'* (BBC News, 19 March 2018)[13]. They are regularly moved from place to place to make it difficult for them to settle and integrate into the local community so that they may give up and return to their country of origin.

The worst human rights violation, which has been condemned by human rights activists as unfair and discriminatory, is keeping immigrants in detention centres. Statistics revealed by these human rights activists claim that at any given point in time, there are some 2,500 asylum seekers being held in detention centres, up to 26,500 each year. The government justifies this policy by arguing that they want to ascertain the asylum seeker's identity or the validity of their claim; to effect their removal from the UK when need arises; and to mitigate the risk of self-harm, absconding or engaging in criminal activities. While Home Office claims may be true, the major reason why people turn to crime is to seek for means of survival. There is also evidence to suggest asylum seekers can be kept in detention centres simply because this is the only type of accommodation which is available. As confirmed by May Bulman, Social Affairs Correspondent for *The Independent*, this practice has been upheld by the Home Office. *'Immigrants are being left to "languish" in removal centres for months on end after being granted bail because the Home Office is refusing to fulfil its duty to provide asylum accommodation, claiming emergency housing is "not dissimilar" to detention.'* (*The Independent*, 27 May 2018)[14].

I remember having to share a house with asylum seekers from different countries. There were people from four different countries and it was impossible to communicate effectively, as we spoke different languages. We could have helped each other to settle down more quickly if we had shared a common language and culture. I felt as though the government was deliberately isolating me by separating me from my culture and social network. I felt like a nomad, moving from house to house. They moved me six times. I could not give my address to family members or anyone with confidence because we did not know when we would be moved to another location that we did not know. As a result, letters often went missing and personal data was put at risk.

The quality of my accommodation was very poor. I had to rely on handouts from charitable bodies and local people to provide suitable furniture and facilities to meet my needs. I was fortunate to flee here without children. I came across families who were also placed in accommodation that was not fit for purpose. Women who have suffered major traumas such as rape and torture are put in properties without adequate security. Children are obliged to live in properties without gardens or play areas. The problem is accurately summarised in the following remark by Maurice Wren, the chief executive of the Refugee Council: *'All too often, people seeking asylum in the UK are forced to live in squalid, unsafe, slum housing conditions, at exorbitant cost to the public purse. …Though the general public is largely unaware of the appalling conditions into which traumatised people are routinely dumped, ministers and officials are not, yet this scandal continues unchecked. The time has come to end this shameful practice and allow people seeking asylum to live in dignity.'* (*The Guardian* 27 October 2017)[15].

A recent report by the Independent Chief Inspector of Borders and Immigration has further confirmed the seriousness of the housing problems faced by asylum seekers. The report confirmed that the majority of state-run accommodation for asylum seekers continues to be sub-standard. The report found evidence of damp, dirty and vermin-infested properties. The dampness and ventilation in one of the properties inspected was so poor that it caused a three-year-old child to suffer health problems. This was verified in a letter issued by the NHS. Women and children were also exposed to harm by being placed in the same properties as men with alcohol and drug problems. This inspection of asylum seekers' accommodation, carried out as recently as 2018, shows that things have not improved much since my own experience with the asylum system between 2002 and 2010. The report makes grim reading and has been corroborated by other studies, which have found that the government's dispersal policy has made the plight of asylum seekers worse. As a matter of government policy, asylum seekers are sent to areas of social deprivation and poor quality, council-owned housing that is not attractive to the local population[16].

In my view, integration means that the local community should be prepared to welcome us. Apart from being placed in an area without social networks, living among people from varied cultural backgrounds, the challenge to settle down and integrate into the local community became even more daunting. The government's failure to prepare local people to welcome immigrants and tolerate them worsened our situation. It took a very long time for me to settle down in the area where I was assigned. I tried to befriend my neighbours but my efforts were often rebuffed. As a black woman with no obvious sign of wealth, I was not accepted. I later learned from the media that many local people see asylum seekers as dangerous. Some see them as threats to their very existence as they are seen as a burden on the state – putting further pressures on housing, education, healthcare and other social services. Asylum seekers are perceived as jumping the queue for social housing and other benefits.

This scenario contradicts government policy of preventing asylum seekers from working before they are granted asylum status and these claims are far from true. If more was done by the Home Office, other central government departments and local Councils to educate the media and local people, many of the integration challenges faced by asylum seekers on a daily basis could be averted. A balanced narrative should explain why asylum seekers flee their countries and should educate people about the gifts they bring with them. Mechanisms should be put in place for local people and asylum seekers to express any fears, concerns or questions, so that these can be addressed in an informed and impartial manner. Opportunities should be provided to facilitate direct contact between asylum seekers and local people. This would promote mutual trust, respect and understanding of each other's culture, needs and expectations. Integration and community cohesion activities could take the form of hosting welcome events for asylum seekers: artistic and sporting events, volunteering opportunities and befriending programmes. The education system, local police force and non-governmental bodies and community organisations such as churches and charities also have a role to play in raising local awareness of the needs of asylum seekers and their potential contribution to their local communities. Initiatives such as Refugee Awareness Week are also helpful in promoting greater community cohesion.

In my view, the other area which I found lacking in my struggle was to do with the housing of asylum seekers. In my experience, asylum seekers are not suitably housed. It is important to provide for their needs in a holistic manner. In fact, in my view, this should be done even before they are housed as it is important to house them where they can easily access the services that are relevant to their needs. For example, the authorities should take their prior education and labour market experiences into account and ensure they are located to areas where they are likely to find jobs that match their skills or access suitable educational opportunities if there are gaps in their education. The Home Office should understand that the needs of asylum seekers vary depending on their country of origin and that the type of pre-asylum traumas they have endured before fleeing from their country are unique. In my view, the Home Office should provide services that take into account cultural and civic training (including language training), social integration support, education, labour market and health.

The Home Office should be aware that each country has its own distinctive norms, cultural traditions and ways of doing things. Even when we share the same language, there are often differences in the meaning of words as well as unfamiliar sayings used in different parts of the host country. Unfortunately, I did not have the benefit of an induction programme to orientate me as to what to expect and how to assimilate the local culture. As I pointed out earlier, although English is widely spoken in Zimbabwe, I felt lost for most of my first ten years of living in the UK. Although I have been living here for 17 years now, I often hear sayings and expressions that I don't understand. I still struggle with understanding regional accents and often have to ask people to repeat themselves multiple times, as much of what they say tends to go over my head.

I had to learn about the local culture by trial and error,

based on what I observed from the way the natives interacted with each other. I naturally learned from the way they behaved towards me in my own interactions with them. I wish there were structured courses to educate me into the local culture and help me to adapt. I know families who have unintentionally broken the law by engaging in cultural practices that are normal in their country of origin but which are illegal here. This includes practices such as using force in resolving domestic conflicts or in the way children are disciplined for unacceptable behaviour. In Zimbabwe, for example, it is a common and universally accepted practice to punish children by smacking them. Men often beat their partners and this, too, is socially acceptable. Differences of this kind can be explained by providing orientation classes about the laws and expectations of the host country as they apply to parenting and all aspects of living in the UK.

I believe cultural adaptation should be a two-way process. Local people should also be made aware of our culture and ways of doing things. This would speed up the integration process and promote mutual understanding of the different cultures. If such training was in place, I would not have had the problems I had with the Home Office authorities when I failed to make direct eye contact with their staff during interviews. By the same token, I would have known that when communicating with British people, you are expected to look them in the eye.

In the same way as the authorities collect biographical details of migrants on arrival and their reasons for fleeing their country, they should also do a skills audit at the same time to learn about what prior education, qualifications, skills and experience asylum seekers possess. Such an audit could serve the purpose of helping both the asylum seeker and the host country alike. It could serve to identify gaps in the asylum seeker's language and general education level and help providers to devise suitable courses for asylum seekers. It could also help the host country to make better use of the skills and experience which asylum seekers bring, thus alleviating labour market bottlenecks. In the absence of a skills audit upon arrival, it is easy for the media and local people to stereotype asylum seekers and make erroneous assumptions, such as that asylum seekers are unskilled and are a burden to the state. The truth is asylum seekers are a heterogeneous group of people. They come to the UK with a variety of skills and experience. Within this group, there are entrepreneurs, doctors, engineers, lawyers, accountants and just about every professional category.

By virtue of their diversity, asylum seekers require different types of help and support when it comes to education and training. One size does not fit all. Those who are educated to degree level will need a different type of support from those with basic or no formal education. Their qualifications and experience also need to be assessed and validated so that these can be recognised by employers and educational institutions. Sometimes this will present difficulties for the host country, as asylum seekers will not always have documents to prove their qualifications. Some have been forced to flee with only the clothes on their backs. This means the host country should be flexible in how they go about assessing and validating people's prior education and learning.

Asylum seekers should also be given information about how to obtain financial and childcare support so that they can access education and training opportunities. I experienced a lot of barriers in my attempt to obtain further education while I was waiting for my asylum application to be processed. I had to rely on my social network and non-governmental organisations to inform me about my rights. My top priority was to improve my written and spoken English. I went to People's College in Nottingham to pursue this goal. Subsequently, I decided to enrol at Derby University to do a course in community development and social policy. Although I went to university for almost three years, I still do not have a certificate to confirm my attendance or level of attainment. When the course administrators found out that I was an asylum seeker and that I was having difficulties paying my fees, they refused to mark my assignments. They also barred me from services such as use of the library.

I tried in vain to obtain funding from government sources. As always, friends and non-governmental bodies were more responsive to my needs. I managed to obtain some support from a Nottingham-based organisation called the Nottingham Black Partnership. Unfortunately, the organisation closed because of funding cuts and I was unable to finish the course. By the time I was removed from the course, I had gained a lot of useful knowledge in my chosen field of study. The knowledge I gained helped me to run successful organisations and deliver many initiatives which I am currently involved in. In my view, an integration strategy also needs to address labour market preparation for asylum seekers and refugees. As an asylum seeker, I was not allowed to work while my asylum application was being processed. This was in spite of having to wait for nearly nine years for my asylum application to be processed.

The other issue the Home Office should appreciate is that I came over to the United Kingdom as a talented entrepreneur with a strong work ethic. I was brought up to be independent. I was very disappointed when the right to work was taken away from me. I had to wait for nearly a decade before I was allowed to work. While I was waiting for my asylum application to be processed, I felt worthless, unfulfilled and lost. I was robbed of my dignity. I was not comfortable to rely on meagre state handouts and food-banks to meet my needs. I felt violated as I lacked the means to support my children with the minimum standard of living they were accustomed to. It was impossible to save and plan for the future. I could not afford to keep in regular contact with my family in Zimbabwe as I was forced to live on just over £5 per day. It was impossible to pay for international telephone calls, to buy food, clothes and toiletries and still afford to meet all my other needs from this small state hand-out, including paying for commuting.

One set of crucial information I found out long after I

gained refugee status is that the Authorities should have allowed me to work, because my asylum claim dragged for a very long time through no fault of mine. I was not aware of my rights and the Home Office did not inform me that I had the right to apply for a work permit to work in certain specified jobs if my asylum claim took more than six months to process. I now realise that my human right was violated. Article 23 (1) of the Universal Declaration of Human Rights states Everyone has a right to work, to free choice of employment, to just and favourable conditions of work and to protection against unemployment.' At the very least, people who are skilled and highly qualified and who have good reasons for seeking asylum should be given job preparation training and allowed to work at the earliest opportunity. There is a strong economic and humanitarian case for this. Work gives meaning and fulfilment to people's lives. It allows asylum seekers to integrate well into their new community. It reduces the risk of health problems and places fewer burdens on the National Health Service and the benefits system. Asylum seekers can also help to alleviate skill shortages in the host society. Many asylum seekers are graduates and are trained in areas such as medicine, engineering, accountancy and information technology.

Many of the labour market problems which asylum seekers face once refugee status is granted would probably not exist if more effort was put into employment preparation on their arrival in the UK. There is a body of research evidence which shows refugees face barriers such as discrimination from employers, failure to recognise their qualifications and experience, gaps in their CV, lack of recent work experience or UK work experience, difficulties in obtaining references, confusion over refugees' legal status, their lack of help with childcare, and language difficulties. Kidreab Kidane, an Eritrean refugee with 20 years' experience as an accountant and auditor, highlights the plight faced by refugees in the labour market. Upon fleeing to the UK in 2009, Kidreab faced mounting barriers in his quest to find employment. She is quoted as saying:

'I was much traumatised, being forced to claim asylum because of persecution and here without my family ... Finding a place to live, trying to reunite my family and the stress of trying to find a job with no help in a strange country is not easy. I had no assistance; in fact I had constant pressure from Jobcentre Plus to find any job – with no UK work references and not knowing about the way that UK employers recruit. ... I wasn't getting any interviews and didn't really know where to start. I was expected to restart my career as soon as possible with no integration support from any statutory bodies. Employers don't know what refugee status is, and don't value my overseas experience.'(Chartered Management Institute Insights/News, October 2015).

Examples of asylum seekers whose skills were wasted in the period they were waiting for their papers to be processed are too many to mention. Wahid Ahmad from Afghanistan worked as a civil engineer in his country but ended up as a shelf stacker in London. Iftikhar-ul-haq Khan was a

Supreme Court lawyer and adviser to the United Nations in Pakistan before he sought asylum in the UK. He ended up as a volunteer in the Citizens Advice Bureau in Liverpool. Tiegisty Kibrom, an IT graduate who fled from Eritrea, had to content herself with working as a hotel cleaner in London in spite of receiving a distinction in computing sciences. Tiegisty sums up her disappointment by saying: *'I was expecting I'd get a better job. I am not ashamed to do a cleaning job. It just embarrasses me that, with all my skills, I can't find a single opportunity to work in my field. ... The work is hard. Sometimes you feel abused. They say: "If you don't do this, we will sack you." I have enough stress in my life. They say: "You know, girls, you have to be more grateful. Some people don't have any jobs."'* (*The Guardian*, 8 March 2014)[17].

In the absence of labour market help and support from the state, some asylum seekers resort to illegal working where they are often exploited. In my view, the government should grant asylum seekers the right to work after they have undergone suitable employment preparation training. After spending a year in the host country, it is reasonable for people who used to work before they fled to the UK to at least have the right to work or do voluntary work to keep their skills up-to-date and to refresh their CV. This is not only good for the asylum seeker, but it also makes good business sense for the economy. A study conducted by the Lift the Ban Coalition, a group of 65 organisations, found that the government could recoup £42.4m through tax, national insurance payments and savings on financial support if 50 per cent of the people seeking asylum were allowed to work.

Asylum seekers are also at a disadvantage when it comes to accessing health services. Any meaningful integration strategy also needs to address this problem. It should recognise that many asylum seekers come to the UK with poor health because of the past traumas which they suffered. Some are victims of torture, war, rape, human rights violation, domestic violence and other shocking incidents which have damaged their physical and mental health. Trauma symptoms such as malnutrition, anaemia, anxiety, depression and post-traumatic stress disorder are often widespread. As a priority, their health should be assessed upon arrival in the UK and a care plan should be put in place for them. Unless their health needs are properly met, it is more difficult for asylum seekers to integrate into the host country. Poor health makes it difficult to attend educational institutions, find and keep work, and participate in community activities. Evidence also shows that lack of integration services coupled with harsh asylum policies further aggravates the health problems of asylum seekers. Long periods of waiting for their asylum claims to be processed often leads to anxiety and other mental health problems. Placing them in detention centres and the regime of frequent reporting at reporting centres also affect their health adversely.

Yet asylum seekers often face barriers to accessing healthcare. Many are unable to access basic services even when they are seriously ill. This may be due to problems such as a lack of information about their rights, NHS charging policy, lack of money to pay for prescriptions and/or to travel to GP surgeries and hospitals, negative attitudes of NHS staff and lack of training about asylum seekers' entitlement to healthcare, language difficulties and/or under-provision of interpreting services, and even low confidence and self-esteem. Asylum seekers with failed applications may have fears about being arrested, as members of the police force and Home Office representatives are often present in hospitals. Pregnant asylum seekers have been forced to go without maternity support for this reason. One asylum seeker said: *'I never received any maternity care, nor any other care in general during my pregnancy. I was so scared I didn't ask about pregnancy care. Being part of the system would enable charges to be brought against me.'* ('Asylum seekers in Britain unable to access healthcare', Equality and Human Rights Commission, 29 Nov 2018).

Some asylum seekers even end up dying from their illness because of this fear. To prevent people from going without healthcare because of fear of arrest or forcible deportation, the Chief Executive of the Equality and Human Rights Commission, Rebecca Hilsenrath, has called for the healthcare system to be separated from the immigration system: *'Everyone should have access to good quality healthcare, regardless of who they are and where they come from. People seeking and refused asylums are likely to have particular health needs because of past distressing experiences and the traumatic effects of fleeing to a different country. It's therefore crucial that they are able to fully and easily access healthcare and that their rights are protected by keeping healthcare separate from immigration enforcement. This is just about common humanity.'* ('Asylum seekers in Britain unable to access healthcare', Equality and Human Rights Commission, 29 Nov 2018).

In my view, integration policies should be shaped by the experiences of asylum seekers and refugees, and take full account of their needs throughout the whole asylum process. It also needs to prepare asylum seekers to integrate into the society and to enable them to make the greatest possible contribution while they are in the UK. This could be done from the moment asylum seekers enter the country. The earlier they are helped to settle and integrate, the greater the contribution they are able to make to the host country.

Although I seemed to focus more on the needs of asylum seekers in this chapter, there are other areas where government needs to do more. For example, government needs to develop suitable policies to support the integration of refugees into the society once asylum seekers are given refugee status. Many of the issues that I have discussed above also apply to refugees. Although in theory, refugees have almost the same broad rights as UK citizens, in practice they face discriminatory policies. Upon gaining refugee status, you lose your accommodation and financial support after 28 days. The lack of integration policies and suitable services to meet their needs means that many refugees become homeless and further marginalised at this crucial stage.

Refugees are often overwhelmed by the level of bureaucracy and the complex rules that surround their entitlements. Lack of clear guidance in plain English that they can understand makes it difficult for them to find a new home, claim benefits, access education and training, access free healthcare, find employment, start a business, reunite with their children and other close family members, open a bank account and get a National Insurance number. Without a National Insurance number, it is difficult to claim benefits and seek employment. Yet they are not automatically provided with a National Insurance number at the point at which refugee status is granted. They typically have to wait for a month to obtain their National Insurance number. Many face another round of destitution during this period.

Some refugees even face problems opening bank accounts, without which it is difficult to obtain any social security benefits for which they are entitled. Many lack the type of identification documents which banks require before they allow anyone to open a bank account. Due to administrative oversight, the Home Office sometimes fails to issue new refugees with a Biometric Residence Permit when they are notified about their refugee status. This document provides valid proof of the right of a refugee to live and work in the UK, usually for a period of five years.

The following remark from Alex Fraser, Director of Refugee Support at British Red Cross, summarises the reality faced by many refugees across the UK: *'No one who has fled conflict and persecution should be left destitute as a side effect of being granted protection in this country. Not only does destitution severely impact a person's ability to provide for themselves and their family, but in our experience can also lead to an increased risk of exploitation. Through our front line services, we know that after being given refugee status, the process of finding work and somewhere to live often takes much longer than 28 days.[18]'*

Scotland can be commended for developing an effective strategy for welcoming and integrating asylum seekers and refugees. The strategy is based on a whole system approach, involving all the organisations involved in the provision and delivery of services to asylum seekers and refugees. Significantly, it is also shaped by asylum seekers and refugees. Angela Constance, the Cabinet Secretary for Communities, Social Security and Equalities, is quoted in the New Scots: refugee integration strategy 2018-2022, saying:

'I am proud that Scotland has become home to people from all over the world seeking safety. Scottish Ministers have always been clear that people who seek asylum in Scotland should be welcomed and supported to integrate into our communities from day one. When refugees and asylum seekers arrive, they need understanding, support and hope for their future; and children should be able to be children, whether they arrive with their family or on their own ... New Scots recognises that refugees and asylum seekers face challenges which can limit their inclusion in our society, but it also recognises that refugees bring strength, knowledge and skills. They are assets

to our communities and, as they rebuild their lives here, they help to make Scotland stronger, more compassionate and more successful as a nation.'

Scotland recognises that empowerment and engagement of people seeking sanctuary is a win-win outcome for everyone. By helping asylum seekers and refugees to settle quickly and integrate effectively into their new community, this helps them to overcome pre-migration traumas and release their potential for the benefit of the host community. The rest of the UK needs to learn from Scotland's example. Its vision for the integration of asylum seekers and refugees is set out in the box below.

Looking at all these experiences, one feels that far more needs to be done to provide support to asylum seekers from the moment they arrive in the country. An induction policy should be put in place and they should be informed about their rights in the areas of language training, civic and cultural training, education, housing, employment, healthcare, benefits and other services to facilitate their speedy integration into the society. The needs of refugees should also be addressed. It is not sufficient to give them refugee status after an arduous ordeal without preparing them to settle down quickly so that they can make a positive contribution to their new country. More thought needs to be given to orientation projects. Guidance should also be written in different languages to help asylum seekers and refugees with their integration, and to signpost them to relevant services and organisations which can help to meet their needs throughout the asylum process.

Scotland's Vision for the Integration of Asylum Seekers and Refugees

Vision – For a welcoming Scotland where refugees and asylum seekers are able to rebuild their lives from the day they arrive. To achieve this vision, we will work to ensure that Scotland:

- Is a place of safety for everyone, where people are able to live free from persecution as valued members of communities.
- Enables everyone to pursue their ambitions through education, employment, culture and leisure activities.
- Has strong, inclusive and resilient communities, where everyone is able to access the support and services they need and is able to exercise their rights.
- Is a country that values diversity, where people are able to use and share their culture, skills and experiences, as they build strong relationships and connections.

Source: New Scots Refugee Integration Strategy 2018 – 2022, p.10.

Although I faced these problems, which I shared with other asylum seekers, my plight would have been a lot more difficult had it not been for the generous support I received from friends and my wider social network. I developed good relations with people in non-governmental organisations created to help asylum seekers and refugees to integrate into the community. Among the more notable organisations were the Church of England, Pentecostal Churches and other Faith Bodies, the Refugee Forum and the Nottingham Black Partnership. I recall there were lots of asylum-seekers roaming the streets of Nottingham with no clear goals and nowhere to go to access services.

In the next chapter, I will discuss how the government's unwelcoming and 'hostile asylum environment' affected my health and general well-being. I will also discuss in more detail how my social network and organisations like the Refugee Forum, Nottingham City of Sanctuary and faith agencies helped me and other destitute asylum seekers whose needs were neglected by the immigration authorities. Without their help, further damage would have been done to our health and the cultural and integration challenges would have been insuperable. They tried to understand our needs, treated us with respect and dignity, provided us with food, clothing, counselling and moral support, helped us to understand our rights and entitlements to services, and made it easier for us to adapt to our new environment. I am deeply grateful to these kind people and to their organisations. I will forever be indebted to them.

CHAPTER SIX

SOCIAL ISOLATION AND MENTAL HEALTH IMPACT

It is my contention that asylum system has an negative impact on mental health and the general well-being of people who have gone through this tortuous experience. This chapter builds on the previous chapter by discussing how the asylum system contributed to some extent to my mental health problems as an asylum-seeker and a refugee. This felt like another war of liberation or *Chimurenga* for me. I thought I had experienced the worst abuse in Zimbabwe and I could look forward to living in a safe and dignified manner in the UK; little did I know that I would end up destitute, homeless, isolated and lost by a cruel asylum system that dehumanises asylum seekers and treats them like criminals. The government's policy of hostility and social exclusion of asylum seekers took its toll on my health. It also undermined the mental health of the five young children whom I had left behind in Zimbabwe.

There is a clear and direct relationship between social isolation and mental health problems. These are problems that asylum seekers often experience. Many of us arrive alone and find ourselves without family, friends or any type of social network. This was the position I found myself in during the first four years of my life in Nottingham. Loneliness and feelings of isolation were undoubtedly one of my biggest challenges as an asylum seeker.

I remember the pain and sadness I felt living in shared accommodation with women from other cultural backgrounds and the difficulties of communicating with each other. They were unable to speak English and we had nothing in common, apart from our asylum status. In my first year, I spent most of my time alone in my room, crying and longing for a day when I would be reunited with my family. I missed my husband, young children, extended family and beloved country. Due to lack of resources, I was not able to speak with them for long periods or as often as I wanted.

My pain was made worse as a result of the wider problems I was experiencing in accessing relevant services and integrating into the community. I was not happy in the house where they placed me. I would often try to avoid the home environment by roaming the streets of Nottingham. That even worsened my situation every time I left the house as I did not feel welcome by the local people. I hardly had any opportunities for meaningful interaction with people in the community. I often felt ashamed when I went to the shops to buy goods and had to present the cashier with an asylum payment card rather than cash. My pre-credited 'Azure card' made my status visible. People in the queue and the shop staff often looked down on me and treated me with disrespect.

I did not come to the UK to rely on state handouts. All I wanted was to be able to begin the process of rebuilding my life. Yet I was prevented from doing this. I wished I could start my fashion design business afresh from day one of my arrival but I was prevented from doing so because I was not allowed to work and live independently like I did in Zimbabwe. In my first few years I spent most days without any clear goals. It was difficult to set goals when so many restrictions were placed on what one could do and when one lacked the resources to do things which others take for granted. Although asylum seekers have rights, the Authorities did not tell us about our legal rights and entitlements under the 1951 UN Refugee Convention and other relevant laws. Instead, all their written and oral communication focused on what we could not do. Every day I found myself waiting on the Authorities for news about my asylum application. I eagerly awaited the arrival of the mail most days.

The situation I found myself in damaged my self-esteem. I felt like an orphan – unwanted, unloved, lost, useless and hopeless. I was not prepared for any of this. Zimbabwe had a very close colonial relationship with the UK. I honestly thought I would be welcomed in the UK. This was a country that I believed in before I took the decision to come here. Little did I know that Britain would be so unwelcoming to people seeking sanctuary, even to those coming from their former colonies.

I prayed and cried constantly. I consoled myself by writing entries in my diary about my feelings. This was my pain relief. I felt nostalgic and would lose myself in thoughts of happier times spent back home with the love and support from my family and community members. I remember back home at the age of 11 years when I wrote a poem in my mother language which I entitled 'nherera zvichengete' which literally means 'orphans do look after themselves'. The rejection and discrimination which I felt in Nottingham led me to write the following poem in 2008 to express some of the emotions which I often felt during the years of limbo.

My Black Hands by Faith Gakanje

My black hands, have worked it all.
They have witnessed my suffering and my endurance.
My heart bleeds as it tells a story of heroism of the pain that everyone overlooks.
But my soul strives for.....am still here, still human, voice of the voiceless.
I tell it now for the rest of my kind who lie in silence.
So now...........this voice I give to them,
I will speak for my people.
For together we are still here, still human.
I wake up every morning before any sane thinks about it.
I go, I walk all in search of a penny,
So I can survive, so I can feed and fend for my large family back home

God bless them.
Do I find one?
When will my suffering end?
Who will take care of my babies? Have I failed them?
Cries the voice of the voiceless.......
I yearn for a belonging, to be around familiar faces,
to be with my family and friends again.
I am alienated.
I am discriminated.
Is it my skin colour?
Is it because of my race or my nationality?
Cries the voice of the voiceless.........
Everyone is busy, going on with their own business,
They pass me by like I am non-existent, perhaps made of ice.
Yes! They see through me.
Still here, still human cries the voice of the voiceless.
I say this because I know I have to fight.
I say it out because no one else will.
I am their voice, I will speak out loud.
I will fight, that's what we black women do, F...I...G...H...T!!!!!
Cries the voice of the voiceless........
The sun is setting.
Time for me to go home, what do I call home?
A bench in the park.
That's my home, that hard bench.
It knows my suffering, it awaits me this night.
Cries the voice of the voiceless.........
I have told it to you,

I will tell it again tomorrow and the day after and the next.
I break the silence.
Through all this can you see?
Still here; still human cries the voice of the voiceless.

I admit that like most asylum seekers, I came to the UK with some pre-existing mental health traumas. I had experienced persecution, domestic violence and other types of abuse. I came in search of safety, peace and healing from my mental scars. I wanted an opportunity to rebuild my life and to feel a sense of belonging to my new community. It never occurred to me that life in the UK would be harsh and would inflict further damage to my mental and physical health. It is my humble submission that government should get rid of the draconian asylum policies and show empathy to the needs of genuine asylum seekers. Numerous studies have shown that these policies are destroying the health of some of the most vulnerable people in our society.

Research in mental health has revealed that asylum seekers and refugees are more likely to experience poor mental health than the local population, including higher rates of depression, PTSD and other anxiety disorders. The increased vulnerability to mental health problems that refugees and asylum seekers face is linked to pre-migration experiences (such as war trauma) and post-migration conditions (such as separation from family, difficulties with asylum procedures and poor housing). Research suggests that asylum seekers are five times more likely to have mental health needs than the general population and more than 61% will experience serious mental distress, and yet these people are less likely to receive support than the general population.

Refugee Action reports that refugees have lack of control over their life, they experience a feeling of uselessness, loss of independence and dignity, financial misery, lack of access to services, prevention from employment, separation from friends and family, threat of deportation and uncertainty about the future. All these emotions aggravate the pre-migration trauma which most asylum seekers experience once they flee their country. The problem is further exacerbated when one is rejected by other large segments of the host country. In addition, I experienced overt discrimination as a black woman. The press did not do any good reporting, either, for the most part; their coverage of asylum seekers and refugees was adverse.

The United Kingdom policies and practices on asylum seekers had a damaging impact on my mental and physical health. For most of the period that I spent waiting for my asylum claim to be processed, I experienced anxiety disorders and depression. I tossed and turned in bed most nights. I often felt anxious in public places when I was in the presence of strangers. I felt as though I was constantly being watched by government agents and would often look behind me to check if anyone was following me. I shook like a leaf on a windy day whenever I came into contact with the police.

I used to dread going to the Reporting Centre in Loughborough. Each time I went I feared the police would detain me. I am particularly grateful to Jonathan, a founding member and Treasurer of Nottingham City of Sanctuary then, who would frequently accompany me to the Reporting Centre to help me to hold my nerve. Jonathan was also one of the people who helped me when the Home Office withdrew my accommodation and other benefits. Jonathan's testimonial below speaks volumes about my experiences.

Jonathan Silvery (Nottingham City of Sanctuary Treasurer)

I met Faith when a group of us were starting a branch of City of Sanctuary in Nottingham. The idea was to provide a welcome to local refugees and asylum seekers. We wanted to work with (and not for) anyone seeking sanctuary here. We therefore welcomed them on our committee.

Faith was one of the first asylum seekers to join the Committee for Nottingham City of Sanctuary. She was a very busy woman then; running her own organisation – African Women's Empowerment Forum. She attended our meetings when she could and brought in other sanctuary seekers. Soon, she was on the national committee.

Before Faith was granted refugee status, she was expected to report to Loughborough as part of enforcement. She did not have resources to travel and was reliant on hand-outs from well-wishers. I volunteered to help Faith to keep her appointments with the Reporting Centre. Every Wednesday of each month, I drove her to and from the Reporting Centre in Loughborough. She was afraid of attending those appointments on her own.

She served on the City of Sanctuary Committee as Events Coordinator. I helped her to find accommodation on one of the many occasions when she was made homeless. Faith may have found English society difficult to enter and understand, but I found that I too was in a different culture, meeting her friends and hearing their outlook. They were busy helping each other: getting a business going, offering a place to stay, and generally supporting one another. I was particularly struck by their cheerfulness; despite their many physical hardships. I was made aware of how lucky we are in Britain to be able to speak freely, without having to guard one's tongue.

The more I heard about the restrictions put on those who had come seeking sanctuary – minimal subsistence, jobs not allowed, constant reporting to the Border Service not knowing whether they would be permitted to leave the office – the more I felt we who are comfortably off should do what we could to make everyone feel at home. This led me to offer Faith part of my allotment in the hope that she would bring other sanctuary seekers in. This was not to be: Faith was far too busy.

What has been brought home to me very powerfully is that, for a bureaucracy, a life only exists if it has been documented. Officialdom says you need an official stamp and a unique number to exist. Without them, you simply do not exist. But life goes on for those who officially don't exist. They have been through levels of difficulty and suffering that most of us *cannot imagine. Yet, they laugh, and play, and fall in and out of love, they set up homes (even if they cannot marry without existing) and do business. What's more, not being allowed to have jobs, some have more time and care both for each other and society as a whole. They are welcome here.*

Indeed as Jonathan testifies I felt ostracised. My young children in Zimbabwe could not understand why I was unable to keep in regular contact with them or why they were unable to settle here with me. The youngest one was only two years old when I fled to the UK. It was impossible to speak to them on the telephone as often as I wanted as I could barely live on my meagre subsistence allowance from the government. Indirectly, the government's policies also damaged my family's health in Zimbabwe.

Although fleeing Zimbabwe was a life or death decision, there were times when I felt guilty and wondered whether it was worth the price we all had to pay. Having to leave my children was the most difficult thing to do in my life. I remember my children waving at me as the car drove off to the airport. I tried at all cost not to break down. I did not want them to feel sad or to think they were not going to see me again for a very long time. Their innocent faces haunted me for a long time. I cannot think of anything more difficult than a mother having to leave her children with no one to give them that motherly love. Although all of my 5 children are now adults, I am still trying to come to terms with this trauma.

After nearly 17 years of separation from each other and numerous Court hearings, my youngest child, Takudzwa Victor, was allowed to join me in the UK in December 2018. This is how he describes the impact of my separation on his health and general well-being. In his own words:

Takudzwa Victor – Impact on My Son

'I did not know my mother and anything about her whereabouts. I became an angry little boy running around my other siblings. I had so many questions that were not properly answered. I was not sure whether my mother was dead or alive. It actually seemed to me that she was dead as I didn't hear much from her and like many other orphans I had met in school I felt vulnerable and bitter. At the age of 4 years I started my early learning (baby class). I was very happy to mix with other school children of my age. However, I would feel miserable each time mothers would come and pick their children up from school. I would get the maid picking me up and taking me home. She was lovely and very kind to me. When we got home she would serve me with sadza (our staple food), vegetables stew or rice. I couldn't answer questions from the public who would constantly ask me about the whereabouts of my mother. It led to confusion as well as brain damage to a greater extent. I was told by my dad that my mother had travelled to the UK, but I didn't understand why. It was an awful feeling that pushed me into mental health instability. I had no solution to a lot of things, hence I developed a condition called 'Grandma's seizure' (a type of

epilepsy). This was like war to me. I went through trauma and identity crisis. I didn't know who my mother was ... My life felt empty. It was hard growing up without a mother and not being able to identify her even if I was lucky enough to see her.'

I have come into contact with many people in Nottingham and other parts of the country that have developed severe mental health problems as a result of the government's policy. Many of these women are still receiving mental health treatment long after they were granted refugee status. For example, I know an asylum seeker who came to the UK as a qualified teacher. Unfortunately, her asylum outcome letter was mislaid for two years as it was sent to one of the many addresses where she had lived while she was waiting for her application to be processed. The frustration from waiting and exclusion from work caused her to develop severe mental health problems. Her physical health also deteriorated. She now suffers from a recurrent heart problem.

The news is full of destitute asylum seekers self-harming and even taking their own life. A well-known case is that of 27-year-old Eyob Tefera, from Ethiopia, who drowned himself in Swansea marina in February 2018. His asylum application was declined twice. He became destitute and homeless after becoming a failed asylum seeker. It is reported he made an earlier attempt to take his own life but was still unable to access suitable mental health support. When he came to the UK, he was suffering from post-traumatic stress after witnessing gross atrocities committed by the Islamic

State group in Libya. The Inquest received a report from a mental health liaison nurse stating Tefera said he was 'tired of life' due to his failed asylum attempts and his 'unsuitable housing situation'. This death could have been avoided.

In June 2018, the *Daily Mail* reported on the death by suicide of four young Eritrean asylum seekers who became overwhelmed by the stress of applying for refugee status and the treatment they received from the immigration authorities[19]. Before their death, they expressed dismay with the absence of government support and their ineligibility to work. Academic studies have also concluded asylum seekers and refugees are more likely to self-harm and complete suicide compared to the UK prison population. This is particularly the case with those asylum seekers who are kept in detention centres[20]. It is estimated that more than 1,500 female asylum seekers are kept in immigration detention centres every year, 'often for indefinite periods and without knowing when they will be released.' Many of these women are victims of sexual and gender-based violence with severe mental health problems. They are often put under suicide watch. One such woman kept in Yarl's Wood Detention Centre reported how she started to 'hear voices' telling her to end her life. She made two attempts to take her own life: *'I just felt like my life had been taken away from me. It was at the weekend, so they put me on constant supervision and told me I would see a doctor in a couple of days. The next day, after they had stopped watching me, I tried again. In the days after I tried to kill myself, I didn't see a doctor at all…It was such a relief to get out of there [Yarl's Wood], but I don't understand why they had to put me through it at all. I hope I will start to feel better soon, but I will never forget Yarl's Wood detention centre.'*

There were times when I found myself in a total state of despair and even wondered about the point of living. After spending a number of years feeling trapped and imprisoned, I finally decided to seek volunteering opportunities. This gave me a sense of purpose and helped me to overcome the boredom I was feeling. After a while I noticed I had more energy and was feeling more positive about life. Both my mental and physical improved markedly. This motivated me to offer my services to more organisations. In the process, my social network also expanded. I ended up serving in at least six organisations. These included the Refugee Forum, Nottingham City of Sanctuary, Nottingham Black Partnership, Save the Children charity shops, Rainbow Project and the African Women's Initiative Support project.

I served these organisations in a variety of roles. These included subject-matter expert on asylum and refugee issues, events management and board-level responsibilities. A number of these organisations were set up in response to the basic needs of asylum seekers and refugees. Around the time they were set up, there was hardly any government infrastructure in place to support asylum seekers and refugees. There were lots of asylum-seekers and refugees roaming the streets of Nottingham with nowhere to go to access services.

After serving as a volunteer for a number of years in a number of the organisations mentioned earlier in this chapter, I decided to set up my own organisation in response to a major gap in the services which were provided to vulnerable African women. People including Reverend Dr Valerie Howe, Dianne Sealy-Skerritt and Trevor Messam saw my potential and encouraged me to follow my passion. There was a need to set up a grass-roots organisation to serve as a genuine voice for the voiceless. In the next chapter, I will discuss in more detail the remit of AWEF and the impact this organisation is having on marginalised women.

I place a huge value on the experience which I gained from the various organisations where I served as a volunteer. Although this was not the same as working and did not always make full use of my skills and experience, it helped me to integrate into the society and acquire some status. When my application for asylum was being processed, I felt isolated and cut off from mainstream society because I was had no right to work or to access higher education; volunteering helped me to undertake training and to acquire skills which helped me to find work once refugee status was acquired.

The rest of this chapter introduces some of the many amazing people who came to my rescue when I was at the lowest point of my life. Had it not been for their care and generosity, I would not have survived my ordeal. I can never repay them for their kindness. As the accounts below show, they provided me with a wide range of support, much of which should normally have been provided by government organisations. I am particularly grateful for the help which they provided in helping me to understand my rights, helping me to understand the culture and the way language is used, accompanying me to meetings with government officials, providing me with moral and emotional support, and ensuring my financial and basic needs were met when the government withdrew my housing support and living allowance.

These wonderful brothers and sisters gave me hope to carry on. Unlike the government authorities, they saw my potential and valued what I could give back to the host community. Without realising it, they helped to shape much of the work I am currently delivering through the African Women's Empowerment Forum and my other organisations. They also helped to equip me with the leadership and management skills I needed to succeed in my organisations. The examples below illustrate how many of these generous people helped me when the asylum system failed me.

Trevor Messam trained me to become an effective leader. When he first referred to me as a leader, I told him I was not a leader as I had no one to lead. He convinced me that I was a 'born leader' and that all my leadership skills were dormant within me and were waiting to be expressed. Apart from coaching and mentoring me, he taught me to chair and facilitate meetings and workshops.

Dianne Sealy-Skerritt, former Equality and Diversity Church of England officer and leader of the Rainbow Project, did a lot to empower me and build my confidence. She believed in me. She was like a sister. She ensured my basic needs were met and regularly provided me with clothes. She would share her best clothes with me – not used and unwanted stuff. If I had an important meeting to attend and did not have anything suitable to wear, she was happy for me to wear anything I wanted from her wardrobe. She remains dear to me and has even accompanied me to Zimbabwe to help me to resolve personal issues.

The Support I received from Reverend Dr Valerie Howe – Founder of Women of Destiny cannot be over emphasised. Her testimonial below sums it up:

The Support from Reverend Dr Valerie Howe – Founder of Women of Destiny

In *2005, after starting Women of Destiny, and the passing of my father, I felt as though I couldn't move forward with this project. However, the Lord spoke through my husband and said, 'Woman Rise Up'. This sent a dagger through my spirit, so I started a charity organisation called, Women of Destiny, which aims to bring healing to hurting, wounded women in the community.*

I was first introduced to Faith in 2007. I would visit and speak with her about her aspirations as an asylum seeker. It soon became clear that Faith had a vision to empower African women in the community. The first few years of her life was made difficult, due to leaving her family behind and not being able to work, due to British restrictions at that time. Our relationship developed over a period of time and because of my experience, she asked if I would attend her Women's meetings which were held at Chaucer Street women centre, Nottingham.

It was a cold winter's morning, when I walked into a room filled with vulnerable women who were hurting. Their faces displayed sadness and disillusionment. These women had come to a country; many had to leave children and husbands behind. There was an airy feeling in the room. All eyes were fixed on me, as if I had all the answers to their problems. However, this gave me an opportunity to share and bring hope in the midst of despair. As the relationship developed, many would share their stories, which were heart-breaking and some of the times, I felt tears filling my eyes, as I had compassion for them. However, I prayed and spoke with them as a group, but also supported individuals. I was concerned about their mental well-being and just wanted to reassure and encourage them as much as I could by visiting and sign-posting them to other agencies.

AWEF along with Women of Destiny has identified the specific needs to meet the African woman's social, physical, psychological, emotional, spiritual and social well-being. This was an opportunity for me to demonstrate the skills and abilities that I had, such as: mentoring, advising, guiding, instructing and teaching, which has been used during Women's workshops and conferences.

Faith has worked alongside Women of Destiny and has provided support and empowerment workshops to vulnerable women. As a community and international leader, I have seen Faith develop during the period when seeking sanctuary.

Faith also gave me the opportunity to engage with the African women, especially during the Leadership program, held in 2015. She's an amazingly selfless woman of faith and determination. You are a Woman of Purpose, Substance, Faith and Power.

Thanks to Faith who allowed me to understand and gain knowledge about Asylum and Refugee Status in Britain and the effect it had on people seeking sanctuary. Faith is a woman of determination, consistency and commitment to what she believes her people needs.

Revd. Dr Valerie Howe

It is difficult to forget Dr Rhoda Madziva. I shall forever be indebted to her for the support she generously gave me. This is what she says about our relationship when I had nowhere to turn to:

Dr Rhoda Madziva

I first met Mrs Faith Gakanje-Ajala in summer 2008, when I was carrying out fieldwork for my PhD study which was concerned with the lived experiences of asylum seeking parents living in the UK while forced apart from their children by immigration laws. By conducting this research, I aimed to gain an in-depth understanding of these parents' lived experiences of being separated from their children as well as to understand the human rights violations they had suffered, both as citizens (in the country of origin) and as asylum seekers (when they moved to the UK).

I got in touch with Faith after a colleague had informed me about her organisation, African Women's Empowerment Forum (AWEF) and the work she was doing to support female asylum seekers in the city, though she was herself also an asylum seeker. When I visited Faith I was particularly taken by her courage, resilience and ability to empower other women asylum seekers while she was herself undergoing similar challenges. Over the years I have attended seminars and workshops as well as giving presentations at some of the events organised by Faith. In this way, Faith's work has played a major role in revealing the many 'borders' that asylum seekers have to cross in a variety of ways and contexts after crossing the main border and the many emotional 'journeys' they have to make following the main journey, which all have a detrimental impact on their physical and mental well-being. Overall Faith should be commended for her work, which over the years has afforded women asylum seekers the platform to reclaim their personhood, dignity and honour.

Below are some of my published work in which I have written about Faith's lived experiences as an asylum seeking mother who endured many years of forced separation from her children under a system which treats those seeking protection as asylum seekers first and parent later (if ever).

Arapiles S. and Madziva R. (2017). 'A dignified standard of living' for asylum seekers? An analysis of the UK's labour market restrictions for asylum-seekers, Refugee Review: Special Focus Labour, Vol. III: 65-81.

Madziva, R. (2016). Transnational parenthood and forced migration: the case of asylum-seeking parents who are forcibly separated from their families by immigration laws, Families, Relationships and Societies: An International journal of research and debate, 5(2): 281-297.

Madziva, R. (2015). A gift exchange relationship? Reflections on doing qualitative research with vulnerable migrants, Families, Relationships and Societies: An International journal of research and debate, 4(3): 465-80.

Madziva, R. and Zontini, E. (2012). Transnational mothering and forced migration: Understanding the experiences OF Zimbabwean mothers in the UK, European Journal of Women's Studies, 19(4):428-443.

Pauline Edwards is a character who always warmed up my heart when I was really down and struggling. This is what she says below:

Pauline Edwards

I now refer to Faith as my sister. I first met her at a network event around 2006. At the time when I met her, she was destitute and homeless. I was absolutely horrified when she told me what she had gone through over the last few years. She was lost. She was in a very sad place. The government stopped her support. She decided to set up an organisation to raise awareness of the plight of asylum seekers. She knew many other people who were in the same position as her. I decided to join her organisation and to support the cause. I wanted to contribute in whatever way I could. By this time she was sleeping in a tiny run-down place where she was working from. It was rented to her for a small fee to run her organisation. I decided to stay with her as I didn't want her to stay in it on her own. It was not safe for a woman to stay there alone. The building had no heating or running water. We both slept rough.

The absence of government services for asylum seekers like her led me to help her. As a woman I felt her pain. I was moved by her needs and the fact she was alone with no family support here. She was a stranger in a strange land. It reminded me of what my parents must have gone through when they first came here from Jamaica during the Windrush era. She faced triple-discrimination and rejection because of her immigration status, gender and race. She was down a lot and would sometimes become tearful. It was heart-breaking for her to leave her children behind and to miss out on their upbringing. She spoke about them constantly. I did my best to lift her spirit and to encourage her to stay positive.

I saw her potential. I liked her fighting spirit and her resilience. She was selfless. She was fighting for others, not just for herself. I admired her courage and strength. She reminded me of Winnie Mandela. She worked very hard in her organisation and in those where she offered volunteering services. She was very visionary and full of energy. I thought she could contribute a lot to the society. She inspired others to do their best. Her personal qualities rubbed off on me in little or no time. I wanted to emulate her and be as strong as her. She inspired me to value who I am and gave me opportunities *in her organisation to grow and develop. We complemented each other well. I helped her to understand English culture and the subtleties of the English Language. I also offered her practical support and helped her to set up the African Women's Employment Forum.*

Faith is a woman of courage, strength and resilience. She is highly regarded by many people and organisations in Nottingham. She is an asset to our country. It is a pity she has been subjected to such an ordeal before she was granted the right to start a new life here. She would have contributed a lot more to our society if this right was granted much earlier. I have seen her suffer for a number of years while she was kept waiting for her application to be processed. It affected her health badly. I wish the government would understand the impact their asylum policies are having on vulnerable people who come here for help after facing horrific traumas in their home countries. I urge them to treat these people in the same way they would like themselves to be treated. They are people like them and their own family.

Dr Olga Bailey, Professor at Nottingham Trent University played such an important role to help me rebuild my life. As her testimonial reveals, she was instrumental in rekindling those skills in me which had become dormant because the asylum system would not allow me to use them. Below is her powerful contribution in her own words.

Dr Olga Bailey @ Professor Nottingham Trent University

I first met Faith at 'Alternative Voices' in 2006, a conference I organized at Nottingham Trent University. At that time Faith was seeking asylum in the UK. Faith and I chatted for a few minutes on common interests relating to issues of women and migration. I was immediately struck by Faith's resilience and fortitude in dealing with the difficult position she found herself in. Faith's ideas and purpose for herself and other women asylum seekers and refugees was truly impressive.

Despite being in the middle of a personal crisis, Faith was able to see a better future for herself and other women in similar situation. Faith demonstrated energy and determination to act and take control of her life, despite being subjected to poverty and destitution after her case for asylum was denied. It's true to say that Faith had a vision on how to change and improve the lives of women in a similar situation. I believe this is not a cliché. Faith is a genuine fighter. She does not take 'no' for an answer and strives for the best outcome the system should provide. Faith is charismatic, confident, and friendly and always maintains her smile, even during difficult times.

*I have witnessed the work done by Faith who has changed the lives of countless women **arriving in** the UK destitute. Many of these women are now part of British society, working, studying and contributing to their communities. Faith helps to nurture women to achieve their best and to trust themselves to achieve, despite many difficulties. Faith has supported women to open their own business and apply for funds to help with various issues – including mental health, business literacy and* *domestic violence – all with the purpose to empower women to have a fair chance to succeed.*

Faith works restlessly to support African women coming to Nottingham. She has expanded her work and influence across the UK and abroad. She now works with many African countries to strive to improve the life of young girls and women. Faith has been recognised as a voice of authority, with the experience and knowledge to speak globally about the needs of African women asylum seekers and refugees. Faith's work has brought her into contact with politicians, the media, NGOs and academia where she has presented her story, which has touched the heart of many people who give their support for the inclusion of asylum seekers and women refugees' into British society.

I feel fortunate to have met Faith all those years ago and have followed her development as a woman in search of her place in society with interest. Meeting Faith I felt compelled to support her work to have a place in British society for asylum seekers and refugees women as valuable individuals to the community. This led me to write an academic piece on the process of creating the African Women's Empowerment Forum – AWEF. The article covered its meaning for the women and its importance in giving them a place to call 'home' amid the lack of many basic needs such as a decent place to live, education, health, access to jobs, and so on. I hope the coverage of Faith's work and team has helped to give more visibility to the cause. Faith has made incredible progress and continues working to change the lives of disenfranchised African women in the UK

and abroad. I have learned a lot from her, feel privileged to
have met her and look forward to continue working with her
in supporting women asylum seekers and refugees in the UK
to take their true place in society.

As Dr Olga Bailey has highlighted, the government
should show empathy to the needs of genuine asylum
seekers. Numerous studies have shown that these policies
are destroying the health of some of the most vulnerable
people in our society. *'Asylum seekers and refugees are*
more likely to experience poor mental health than the local
population, including higher rates of depression, PTSD and
other anxiety disorders. The increased vulnerability to mental
health problems that refugees and asylum seekers face is
linked to pre-migration experiences (such as war trauma)
and post-migration conditions (such as separation from
family, difficulties with asylum procedures and poor housing).
Research suggests that asylum seekers are five times more
likely to have mental health needs than the general population
and more than 61% will experience serious mental distress.
However, data shows that they are less likely to receive support
than the general population.' (Mental Health Foundation)[21].

A similar picture is painted in the aptly labelled report on
Refugee Action[22]. Refugees and asylum seekers lack control
over their life, experiencing feelings of uselessness, loss of
independence and dignity, financial misery, lack of access to
services, prevention from employment and separation from
friends and family. Threat of deportation and uncertainty

about the future can aggravate the pre-migration trauma which most asylum seekers experience once they flee their country. The problem is further aggravated by rejection from large segments of the host country, overt discrimination levelled at black women like myself and adverse press coverage about asylum seekers and refugees. I have seen how these policies and practices have damaged my own mental and physical health.

Had it not been for my volunteering activities, my situation would probably still be in a position where I am waiting for my asylum application to be processed. I know people who have been kept in this precarious and inhume position for over 20 years. The Home Office acknowledged the huge contribution I made to the voluntary sector and took this into account in the decision to give me protection in the UK. Through my volunteering activities, I also developed the confidence to present my case more effectively. I also gained opportunities to meaningfully integrate into the society, learn the language, and develop a better understanding of the cultural norms and practices.

I will never forget the kindness I received from people and Charitable organisations in Nottingham. They remain a part of my journey and continue to support my cause and the work which I am currently engaged in. Now that my status has changed from asylum seeker to refugee, many of them are helping me to maximise my contribution to the UK society and to champion the cause of dispossessed and marginalised women. I no longer feel isolated in the UK. I regard all these wonderful people as part of my extended family.

CHAPTER SEVEN

MY LIFE AS A LEADER AND ENTREPRENEUR

'A woman is the full circle. Within her is the power to create, nurture and transform. '

Diane Mariechild

This chapter discusses how and why I set up the African Women's Empowerment Forum (AWEF) and FaGee Fashions. As 'the voice of the voiceless', I will highlight the impact that AWEF is having on women's confidence and their general well-being. FaGee Fashions provides a practical example of the entrepreneurial potential of women refugees and how entrepreneurship can help them to take control over their lives.

African Women's Empowerment Forum (AWEF)

The first nine years of my life in the UK felt like a nightmare. During those arduous years most of my time and energy was spent struggling to secure asylum and refugee status in United Kingdom. Life was drudgery. Each day was spent in a state of limbo with no clear direction or sense of purpose. This changed once I finally received 'refugee status' towards the end of 2010. This gave me the freedom to use the gifts and talents which I brought to the UK. I came to the UK as an entrepreneur with specialist skills in fashion design. When I landed on UK shore I thought that I would be given the right to live and work here within six months of applying for asylum. I envisaged myself resuming the business activities which I had successfully carried out in Zimbabwe for many years.

My long and arduous asylum experience altered my vision. I remain committed to my fashion design business idea. However, I became conscious of the need to establish an organisation to respond to the concerns and needs of vulnerable, powerless and voiceless women. Most of these women are asylum seekers, refugees and migrants of African origins. These needs were very evident during my asylum years and there was no other organisation responding to it. In spite of their good intentions, there was no one who understood my cultural roots well enough to speak for me. This was further confirmed in a baseline study I conducted before formally setting up The African Women's Empowerment Forum. Among other things, the study found many of the everyday needs of African asylum seekers, refugees and migrants were not adequately provided for. Issues such as ill-health, family separation, destitution, domestic violence, social isolation, poor self-confidence and lack of purpose were widespread. The first 'Mapping Exercise' found trapped women who were forced into prostitution as a means of supporting themselves and their children back home. One woman became HIV-infected in the process.

AWEF was established to make a positive difference to the lives of marginalised African women. It can be seen as a positive that came from my negative experience with the UK asylum system. The organisation, created in 2006, by myself in partnership with a number of other African women from across the continent and who sharing the same vision, came together. I did not have the freedom and personal capacity to pursue its mission with vigour until after 2010 when I received the right to settle and work here indefinitely. The organisation's mission is to champion and promote the interests of all African women and their children so that they can realise their true potential. Our core work is focused on the needs of migrants, refugees and asylum seekers who may need more dynamic and tailored support. The organisation is the voice of the voiceless and represents our members' interests on a wide range of immigration, legal, social, economic, educational, health, housing, cultural and personal development issues.

In addition, this organisation aims to spearhead issues relating to asylum and immigration, gender and domestic violence, safeguarding children's welfare, dealing with pre-migration and post-migration traumas which impact on the women's mental and physical health, acting as a social justice champion. It also seeks to promote African women's rights through the court system, helping them to understand British cultural norms and values, provide mechanisms and opportunities for them to integrate meaningfully into society, and tackle poverty and marginalisation of female migrants. We support women on issues such as separation and breakup of families, family mentoring, mental health support, and other health conditions. Our motto captures the essence of the organisation's purpose – *Educate a woman, empower a nation*. This organisation takes a holistic approach to empowering asylum seekers and refugees.

Empowerment is at the heart of our work programme and values. Nowadays, the word 'empowerment' comes up in almost every conversation relating to women's rights. It is part of the policy agenda of many governments and non-governmental bodies. Some even have departments of women empowerment in place to promote gender equality. This is in recognition of the fact that no country can prosper if it ignores the interests and gifts of more than half of its population. Empowerment for these government and non-governmental bodies is about creating a level playing field so that women can fulfil their potential in all spheres of society. Their programmes emphasise full participation of women in the political and economic life of their country, ownership and control of resources, and opportunities to raise their socio-economic status through education, training, employment and career advancement.

AWEF agrees with this ambitious vision of empowerment for women. However, our vision is more modest as most of our members are starting from a very low base where they have little more than their basic human rights. Many are voiceless and have little direct control over their lives. As marginalised women, the organisation's core priority in the short-term is to gain recognition for the rights of all our members, especially for those who are asylum seekers and refugees. We are fighting for all our women to have their rights recognised so that they can take care of their own needs and fulfil their purpose in life. Our women want to be economically independent and not reliant on hand-outs from the state or anyone else. Dependence on government, organisations or people demotivates women and erodes their confidence. It damages them economically, psychologically, mentally and socially. It also sends the wrong message to the women's children. If not addressed properly, dependence and disempowerment can have negative generational consequences.

Our female asylum seekers have rights under the United Nations Refugee Convention (1951) and the later Protocol (1967). These rights must be recognised in principle and in practice. Any woman with a genuine fear of persecution on grounds of race, religion, nationality, membership of a particular social group or political opinion have the fundamental right to seek asylum in signatory countries. They also have the right to be protected from forced return to places of danger in their country of origin. The host countries where they have sought asylum have a duty and responsibility to provide appropriate services for asylum seekers and refugees. These include the right to free movement, freedom of association, services to integrate them into the host country, the right to healthcare, higher education and, at the very least, preparation for employment.

The organisation is at the forefront in lobbying for the Home Office and other government bodies to listen to the concerns of our members. Some of our vulnerable members are forced to report to reporting centres as part of enforcement even though they are victims of sexual and gender-based violence such as genital mutilation, rape and forced prostitution. Some have been kept in limbo for more than 10 years for their asylum application to be processed. Some are undergoing severe mental health trauma and are at risk of self-harm and suicide. We want our members to be treated like human beings with full recognition of their human rights at the very least.

The organisation seeks to achieve its mission by creating opportunities to support women through empowerment and confidence-building training sessions, mentorship, arts projects and networking. We also support women's development by providing access to suitable development programmes including education, career and business development opportunities. Our empowerment model seeks to give African women, refugees and asylum seekers (as well as their children) the power to make decisions on their own by giving them access to credible information and resources. We encourage our women to think for themselves and to be assertive about their rights. We train them to understand the difference between submissive, aggressive and assertive behaviours.

We adopt an integrated and systemic approach in the way we develop and implement services to promote the advancement of African women within society. Part of our overall social gain agenda is to contribute to positive changes in women's status. We want to see a reduction in gender inequality and an increase in the number of women in leadership positions in UK society. We provide women with the development and the support they need to achieve their goals.

Many of our women struggle with mental and physical health problems as a result of their pre-migration and post-migration experience. Like me, they have had to deal with persecution issues on a horrific scale before they fled to the UK. Since coming to the UK, some have also found themselves homeless, destitute and isolated from their families. They have also faced hate crimes, discrimination from local people, and difficulties in integrating and participating meaningfully in UK society. This experience has left many of our women with a wide range of mental health problems. Some of the more common ones are panic attacks, anxiety disorders, and post- traumatic stress depression.

One of the tools we use to support women and aid their recovery is Wellness Recovery Action Plans (WRAP). WRAP is use to equip the women to take control over and full ownership of their lives, rights and needs. This programme enables them to advocate for themselves and make choices about their lives. It reduces isolation by bringing women together to discuss and to write and share their stories and talk about their feelings. The programme can be seen as a 'talking therapy'. It also helps women to make new friends and develop a fresh network of support to promote community cohesion and integration into the wider society. It nullifies taboos, myths and ingrained beliefs that contribute to hidden in-family abuses against women. WRAP is person-centred. It is built for and around the affected individual, to help them to become aware of their internal strength and personal power. The methodology behind the programme is recognised by the National Health Service.

By raising their self-confidence and self-efficacy, women are empowered to take responsibility for their lives and ward off unwanted abuse. Ultimately, WRAP supports these women to become active participants in the daily life of their community. We want them to move from being a victim to a genuine asset to their new society. We have already seen many of our women helping themselves and reducing their dependence on the NHS, police and social workers.

About my Wellness Recovery Action Plan (WRAP)

Wellness Recovery Action Plan has been developed to facilitate and maintain wellness as a practical, day-to-day means to manage a person's health after the experiences of trauma. WRAP helps individuals to identify the Wellness Tools that will most benefit themselves; they will learn to use these tools whenever they are needed. It helps individuals to notice when things seem to be off balance in their lives, and help them to coordinate effective ways to get back to feeling their best. Key elements of WRAP include:

- Daily Maintenance Plan
- Identifying Triggers and an Action Plan
- Identifying Early Warning Signs and an Action Plan
- Identifying When Things Are Breaking Down and an Action Plan
- Crisis Planning
- Post Crisis Planning
- Knowing what makes an individual happy and managing triggers to avoid crisis

It will help the individuals to:

- decrease and prevent intrusive or troubling feelings and behaviours
- increase personal empowerment
- improve quality of life
- assist in achieving their own life goals and dreams.

The aim is to enable women's resilience and well-being, to use a Wellness Recovery Action Plan (WRAP) approach to address health, family and social issues. It provides an effective, economical and sustainable method for women to address their health matters, especially mental health and self-worth, in their roles as primary caregivers. Experience with women's groups that have been using WRAP in England has shown that prevention is a far better option to recovery and intervention after a breakdown however 'minor'.

The WRAP approach gives people:

- A focus on wellness and strengths, rather than illness and deficits
- Self-management techniques for retaining and/or regaining their sense of well-being
- Ways to identify and access the right support
- Empowerment to cope with their day-to-day lives

The WRAP approach is proving to be an invaluable tool in health education and in raising mental health awareness. Using simple, common sense techniques, such as identifying one's own 'triggers' for mental distress and finding ways to eliminate negative feelings, it can be implemented by ordinary people within their own communities, rather than relying on health professionals. So the WRAP approach allows individuals, families and carers to take their mental well-being into their own hands, and to support others in doing the same. It has been successfully used to engage with communities, especially those considered under-served and marginalised. Evidence for the programme's effectiveness is growing alongside its increasing use, both nationally and internationally. For people who are already experiencing mental health difficulties, it also works well alongside professional interventions and programmes. Its greatest power is its simplicity. *I believe wellness is a choice people*

A LIFE ROBBED

need to make the right choices. If you are part of the problem, aim to be part of the solution.

In 2009–2010 AWEF UK delivered a partnership WRAP Programme funded by the NHS Midlands and developed five facilitators who currently support women refugees and asylum seekers on a voluntary base. AWEF as an organisation is committed to deliver the WRAP way to vulnerable women who have gone through distress/trauma; we are responsible of our wellness.

AWEF is truly an enterprising and innovative organisation. We do not duplicate the services offered by other organisations which provide services to African migrants, asylum seekers and refugees. Our organisation is designed to address a gap in service provision to this group. It is an organisation which is tailored to the needs of African women. Run and governed by African women, we understand our women's needs, cultural practices and expectations. We are therefore able to respond with solutions and services which are tried and tested, and are likely to be owned and accepted by our women.

In the long wait for asylum I was very disheartened by the lack of organisations which genuinely understood our cultural needs and expectations. There were many organisations which were championing our cause and were well-intentioned but they were not always sensitive to our needs. There were times when I found the attitude of people in some of these organisations to be patronising

166

and even downright discriminatory. Things were often done to us, rather than anyone consulting with us about what we needed. When we expressed our views on issues that impacted us, we were not always listened to or treated with respect. Sometimes, without realising it, we were stereotyped and placed in boxes based on people's perceptions of life in our home countries. People in some of these organisations did not realise some of us like myself were forced to give up a home of luxury and comfort for a life of struggle and destitution in Europe in our quest for protection. At times, I found their attitudes to be patronising and insulting.

Members of the organisation who have used our services feel a sense of belonging in our organisation. They know their voices are heard and we are committed to champion their cause. This is the principal reason why our organisation is so popular among women from all backgrounds. We regularly hold 'round-table discussions' and 'focus workshops' with stakeholders from central government, local authorities and non-governmental organisations to address issues affecting the lives of our members. The actual composition of stakeholders depends on the issue in question. For example, we work with the police, NHS and social services departments on female genital mutilation, rape and other gender-based violence issues.

We also lobby the Home Office for reforms of the asylum system. For example, following a legislation passed by the UK Parliament to stop migrants from uniting with their families, AWEF led a national campaign 'Reunite Me

With My Children' in 2011 to challenge this law. Through the 'Reunite Me with my Children' project, we continue to raise awareness of the costs of family breakdown when migrants and people seeking sanctuary are separated from the children who they left behind in their home countries. The project aims to change the immigration rules so that these families can be reunited.

AWEF helps victims of the UK asylum system to get their voice heard. I remember when we decided to help a former migrant who the Home Office claimed was working here illegally. The woman in question came here as a minor and later went on to train as a doctor. She became a qualified mental health consultant in the NHS and had an excellent track-record in the NHS Trust where she was working. The Home Office caught up with her and found she did not have a work permit. They tried to deport her. She was taken to court by the NHS. Our organisation produced a statement to support her claim. AWEF also provided her with moral and practical support. Her employers and the wider community also rallied round her to stop the deportation. The judge threw out the case and ruled in her favour. The judge acknowledged her contribution to the NHS and her potential to give more to the society if given a chance. This is an example of the type of injustice which our women face and the difference the organisation makes to their life.

Although the majority of our members are of African origins, we are happy to welcome all vulnerable women regardless of their race, colour or creed so long as they accept and behave in accordance with our values and code of conduct. We have members from the Middle East, Asia, Europe, Latin America and the Caribbean. Indeed, our current chair for the Nottingham branch of the organisation is a Brazilian, Professor Olga Bailey. We also welcome volunteers from all backgrounds.

We operate on a *'hub and spoke'* model. Our hub or headquarters is in Nottingham. The idea is to create spoke or satellite organisations across the UK and expand overseas using Nottingham African Women's Empowerment Forum (NAWEF) as a template. Each satellite organisation is required to replicate NAWEF's values, working practices and organisational procedures. We rely on grants from Local Authorities and other organisations to fund the organisation's activities. This is supplemented by a yearly subscription from our members as well as income from training events, conferences and workshops. We also host fundraising events such as dinners and auctions.

Within the organisation, members benefit from having access to an extensive social networking, advice and support on immigration issues, community integration processes, Wellness Recovery Action Plan therapy, access to health programmes and counselling, mentoring, advocacy, support and signposting, advice and support on setting up and running different types of businesses, training, career development, coaching and personal development, and discounts to all events, workshops and conferences organised and delivered by the organisation.

Since starting in Nottingham in 2006, we have established chapters in three other UK cities. AWEF also has chapters overseas in Zimbabwe and Nigeria. We regularly receive requests from other parts of the UK and overseas to set up further chapters as the issues we tackle are commonly faced by women from all walks of life and cut across geographical boundaries. As our organisational and funding capacity develops, we will implement our expansion plans so that within the next five years we will have a presence in every region of the UK. We will also establish more overseas chapters based on where the demand for our services is greatest. We are currently doing baseline studies to inform the further roll-out of AWEF.

The organisation prides itself on *learning by doing*. Empowerment is about helping vulnerable people to believe in themselves and giving them the confidence to use their God-given talents. Each person is here because God has given us a unique job to do to make a positive difference to people's lives. We regularly invite female role models to share their journeys with our members and to offer them advice and practical guidance to pursue their calling.

THE ESTABLISHMENT OF FAGEE FASHIONS

Having successfully established AWEF in 2006, I also saw the need to set up a complementary commercial enterprise as soon as I was eligible to do so. This became known as FaGee Fashions and was created in 2010 shortly after I received notice of the right to settle in the United Kingdom. My decision to set up this business was driven by three factors. First, I wanted to recreate the success I had had in running a textiles and fashion business in Zimbabwe before I fled the country. Second, I wanted to lead by example and show members of AWEF what empowerment means in practice. I wanted to 'walk my talk' so that the women could see that anything is possible if they are prepared to develop a vision and work hard to turn their vision into reality. Third, I wanted to have an organisation where African women could learn and gain from my expertise and example. I wanted to be able to give them volunteering experience and opportunities to learn about the textile and fashion business. I also wanted them to learn leadership and other business skills so that they would be empowered to set up and run their own organisations.

I formed FaGee Fashions as a Community Interest Company as I wanted all profits to be channelled back into the organisation to develop it for good social causes. I see the business as a complementary arm of AWEF. It helps to reinforce AWEF's remit and funds many of its activities. I am grateful to all those who played a part in helping me to make the business a reality. My biggest challenge in the beginning was funding. I owe a huge debt to the Rayne Foundation. Following my success in a competition that we entered, the Rayne Foundation provided me with a grant to develop and implement my business idea. I am also grateful to The Enterprise Refugee Network (TERN) for a range of business supports, including training, mentoring and funding. This support from TERN is ongoing.

Fagee Fashions
Bringing Colours to British Society

Juliet Line

A key member of the refugee community in Nottingham has been awarded a Fellowship by the Rayne Foundation. Faith Gakanje was selected for the Fellowship for her entrepreneurial idea, Fagee Fashions. The Fellowships are designed to give refugees living in the UK who have a 'Big Idea' the opportunity to turn their vision into reality.

The year-long programme will provide Faith with support, resources and training in the art of doing business, ensuring the successful development of Fagee Fashions.

As part of the learning process, Faith will be visiting Cox's Creation Project in The Gambia to gain more in-depth knowledge of a project similar in operation to that of Fagee Fashions. Cox's Creation Project is a fashion design project in The Gambia that provides training for girls who have never been to school.

"Going to the Gambia will be my first point of learning. I look forward to working with girls who are disadvantaged, who are also developing sewing skills and to having the opportunity to share my knowledge of the industry with them."

66

Fagee fashions will deliver integrated fashions from an African perspective 99

For more information about Fagee Fashions email: fageefashions@ymail.com

FaGee Fashions prides itself in integrating African patterns and fabrics with British styles. The company produces a wide range of clothing for women, men, young people and children. Based on the market research that I carried out, I found young British people with African heritage had a need for modern fashions that connect them to their roots. The company's brand symbolises my vision of our shared future – different cultures and traditions coming together to create something new, special and beautiful.

The company currently operates in the UK, Gambia, Nigeria and Zimbabwe. I am currently working with TERN and my advisors to expand the company's operations. My vision is to locate the business on the high street alongside other household clothing businesses like Marks &Spencer, House of Fraser and NEXT. Currently, much of the production for the UK arm of the business is carried out from a spare room in my home. Work is also carried out in the Gambia, Zimbabwe and Nigeria. Raw materials are mainly sourced in these countries. The products are sold online and through retail outlets and private individuals. We also produce bespoke clothing to meet the needs of individuals. This includes clothes for special occasions, such as weddings and baptisms. (image 9 - Faith TERN)

The company provides employment opportunities for African migrant women and those who have been given refugee status. The company offers work experience, volunteering opportunities and mentoring to women and young people. We help women to set up their own businesses. From time to time, we run fashion workshops where we train people in the art of pattern drafting, cutting to measure and sewing their own garments.

AWEF and FaGee Fashions have already helped a large number of women and their children to gain respect and dignity, secure their rights, develop their confidence, improve their health and increase their participation in their community. We have helped women to gain a stake in UK society through becoming trained and educated, obtaining the right to settle here and to contribute positively to the economy through gainful employment and setting up their own businesses, and reducing their dependency on state benefits and hand-outs from charity organisations and private donors. We have also helped to reduce gender violence within families and to bring about stronger and more cohesive family units. We continue to participate in international forums and work across European countries, advocating on issues of migration impact, asylum, poverty and women empowerment.

AWEF's services are highly valued by members. Its impact has been widely recognised by funding bodies and stakeholders. Without their support, we could not have made the achievements we have so far recorded. Readers can learn more about our activities and success stories by visiting our website and follow us on our social media platforms. Our website address is www.awef.org.uk.

AWEF also operates a hotline number (078 1749 1008) that is available 24 hours a day (all year round) to dispense advice, information and support to our members on any issues or concerns they may have. Our staff and volunteers are trained to give advice and support on immigration, housing, health, domestic violence, law and order, and a wide range of other issues which affect migrant women, refugees and people seeking sanctuary. With more resources we could help a lot more women. Our vision is for AWEF to be present and active in every region and major city of the UK so that African women can feel a sense of belonging and get timely access to the help and support they need.

Although I find myself playing 'catch up', I am proud of

what I have achieved since I gained the right to settle here. My greatest achievement to date since arriving in the United Kingdom is the founding of AWEF and FaGee Fashions. I am also proud of the various campaigns that I have run to enable black women to remain in the UK, get a job, apply for education and get their children out of detention centres. I could have achieved far more to help myself and other vulnerable women had the Home Office accepted my case for asylum earlier. My contribution to UK society could have been far greater.

Through the programmes delivered by AWEF and the operations of FaGee Fashions, my vision is to raise government awareness of the rich potential of migrants, asylum seekers and refugees. Above all, I want policy makers and funding bodies to be better informed of the entrepreneurial capacity of this much-neglected group of people. Asylum seekers and refugees are highly motivated and resilient people. These are precisely the qualities needed to become successful entrepreneurs.

The entrepreneurial potential of refugees is comprehensively assessed and documented in a recent report produced by the Centre for Entrepreneurs. The report makes the insightful observation: *'Each generation of refugees has made significant contributions to the UK, and their collective impact can still be found on the high street today. Michael Marks of Marks & Spencer and Montague Burton of Burton Group were among the Jews who fled the Russian pogroms in the late nineteenth century. In the1950s, Lakshmishankar and Shanta Pathak fled Kenya and set up the much-loved Patak's curry brand. Ugandan Asian refugees are to thank for bringing Domino's Pizza to the UK and for launching Tilda rice. The list goes on.'*(Centre for Entrepreneurs, *Starting Afresh*, March 2018).

CASE STUDY

**FAITH GAKANJE-AJALA
FAGEE FASHIONS**

From taking part in the liberation of Zimbabwe at age nine, to starting a new life in the UK 25 years later, Faith Gakanje-Ajala has faced her fair share of adversity. The owner of a thriving textiles business, she was forced to leave it all behind after becoming the target of government violence. But despite having her application rejected five times and waiting nearly eight years for asylum in the UK, Faith never lost hope: now a graduate of TERN's incubator, not only is she recreating her previous success, but is helping other African women along the way.

I am also pleased to see that there are many examples from around the world where policy makers are creating opportunities for refugees to express their creative and enterprise abilities. For example, the European Commission has established a €3 billion Asylum, Migration and

Integration Fund with part of this sum earmarked for labour market integration programmes and entrepreneurship development projects (AMIF). The UK government needs to put in place similar initiatives to help asylum seekers and refugees realise their potential to establish and run successful businesses.

Both AMEF and FaGee Fashions will continue to work tirelessly to champion the interests of migrants, asylum seekers and refugees. We will ensure the right infrastructure is put in place to fund and support businesses from this group of talented people. Helping asylum seekers and refugees to run their own businesses will offer many benefits to the individuals themselves and to the wider society. It will help them to generate their own sources of income and overcome many of the barriers they face in looking for employment. It will give them a stake in the host country and aid their integration into the wider society.

This chapter concludes with a few testimonials from people who are familiar with the work of AWEF and FaGee Fashions. The testimonials are a testament to the impact that these organisations are having on the lives of disadvantaged women and the wider UK society. I am grateful for the love and support of all these amazing brothers and sisters. Words of encouragement like these keep me going and provide the inspiration for me to press on in my mission to make empowerment of African women a reality.

COMMENDATIONS FOR
AWEF AND FAGEE FASHIONS

The first commendation came from Professor O.A. Ajala who wrote as follows:

Professor O.A. Ajala – Faith: A Refugee Moved By Faith
I met Mrs Faith Gakanje-Ajala by accident on Facebook in 2008 while I was advocating about the plight of Teenage Mothers in my local community (Modakeke, Osun State, Nigeria).She read about a small piece on the issues of Teenage Mothers in Modakeke Community and she was fascinated to know more about their cases. She then contacted me; thus we started interaction and sharing of ideas, stories and aspirations.

She narrated her story and journey of life. I felt elated about her struggle from childhood in Zimbabwe, her political struggle against the tyranny of Government of the maximum ruler (Robert Mugabe) as it affects, particularly women. Her struggle earned her political persecution to the extent that she had to escape for her life. Since then, I have been supporting her work as a mentor at professional level as academic. She left Zimbabwe in 2002 as a political refugee for United Kingdom without any iota of what the future holds for her in a foreign land, except her faith according to her name.

In the UK, she faced initial challenges of language barrier, cultural norms, social isolation, destitution, misconceptions about asylum seekers, racial and gender discrimination and lots more. By faith, she forged ahead without wavering. She was eventually granted refugee status after over eight years of struggle in the United Kingdom. She summoned courage to turn her situation around for the success story that we have witnessed in this last decade. By her faith and struggle, people come to appreciate her for her doggedness. She was accepted with love by new friends and found her feet again.

Through the establishment of AWEF and FaGee Fashions, she became a rallying point for other political and economic refugees not only in the UK but the entire Europe. She became a voice for voiceless women, she engaged government institutions, and she continues to fight for the rights of underprivileged women in society.

In 2016 February, Faith visited my family in Nigeria on a short holiday. Our discussion at that time led to the vision of establishing chapters of AWEF in other countries of Africa starting from Zimbabwe which has already taken off, followed by Nigeria and others. Apart from her effort in helping poor women in her home country, in 2017/2018 she extended the operation of AWEF to Zimbabwe where she established a chapter to lend a helping hand to empower women in local communities. She is also in the process of establishing a chapter in Nigeria which we are working on collaboratively.

It is, indeed, a good step for her to put her experience down in a book which could serve as motivation for others in a similar situation as she was in. The book will provide vital information for asylum seekers on what opportunities abound and the challenges to overcome in their effort to settle down in a foreign land. I highly recommend the book for African Women and all who are faced with migration challenges and social injustice. The book portrays a life of faith, courage and hope. Her experience shows there is no challenge that is too difficult to overcome, The message for everyone is – keep going, have faith, be courageous, never take your eyes off your goals and always keep hope alive.

Dianne Skerritt summarised our efforts to pick up every woman from the doldrums to be a better person who is respected by society at large. She wrote:

Dianne Skerritt – Social Justice Champion and Author of When God Calls

I first met Faith in 2007 at a Refugee Awareness Week planning meeting when I was responsible for managing the Rainbow Project. We bonded very quickly and this was the beginning of a very good, long and fruitful relationship. It was clear from the beginning that she was visionary and wanted to do a lot to improve the lives of marginalised women. She was an example of someone whose needs have been overlooked by government policy makers. Even though she was still an asylum seeker at the time when we met, her main focus was to find a solution to the problems.

This led her to set up AWEF, which became the voice for voiceless women, most of whom came from Africa. She created a culture within AWEF where women are encouraged to think for themselves, celebrate their gifts, find solutions to problems which affect them, and work together to support each other.

I was struck by Faith's courage, resilience and leadership skills. It was clear she had a lot to offer to our society. She showed good networking skills and was very loyal to the women. She was always there when they needed her. She does not suffer fools gladly and functions at a very fast pace. Due to her drive and understanding of what it takes to be successful, Faith sometimes find it difficult to work with those who cannot work at her pace or those who cannot see the opportunity in every situation.

It is these personal traits which led her to progress to setting up her clothing company, Fagee Fashions, within months of gaining the right to settle in the UK. Those who know of this company can see and understand the passion and creativity that is displayed in her beautifully designed clothing range. Anyone who has the opportunity to wear a FAGEE outfit (as I have done on so many occasions) knows the care, comfort and creativity that comes with it.

I feel honoured to have been invited to be part of Faith's journey, both personally and professionally. It has been a pleasure being a part of her life during the valleys and mountains. I will always treasure memories of the times I spent caring about her needs and working with her on services to meet the needs of people seeking sanctuary. I am proud to know her and her family. It gives me immense pleasure to watch her grow. I expect her book to be a blessing to many people. It will give readers an insight into what makes her succeed even when the odds are stacked against her. One clear lesson from her life is that we should keep on pursuing our goals no matter what obstacles we face. So long as we don't give up, we will eventually succeed.

Dr Maggie O'Neill made these recommendations about me and this manuscript, which I am compiling into a book:

Dr Maggie O'Neill

I write this contribution to Faith Gakanje's book on International Women's Day 2019. It is very appropriate to do so. Faith is an amazing woman, a leader, and creative and offers incredible support for other women. Faith was a community co-researcher on an AHRC-funded knowledge exchange research programme in the East Midlands that I led with Phil Hubbard. Faith worked and walked with us, Nottingham City Arts, Charnwood Arts, Artists in Exile and other arts and community organisations supporting women seeking asylum and refuge in the UK. It was a privilege to work with her in support of all those seeing Asylum and Refuge in the East Midlands, UK

Kelbert Henriques – Information Technology Specialist also says this about my effort to reach out to women of all backgrounds:

Kelbert Henriques – Information Technology Specialist

I have known Faith for well over twelve years now. I first met her when I was a Director of Learn and ACE Consortium. At that time she was a volunteer with The Nottingham Black Partnership. I have been supporting her social enterprise and wider community activities since 2010. My services to her range from mentor to advisor. I enable her to develop many of the good ideas she brings to the table and help her to put them into practice. You could say that I walk Faith's journey with her or you could say that Faith pulls me along her journeys, even if I am sometimes reluctant to do so. She is a gritty person who doesn't take no for an answer. If she wants something she does not stop until she achieves it. This is not intended as a criticism. It is a tribute to her resilience and determination in pursuance of her goals until they are achieved.

Faith has great potential in delivering huge social and economic gains. However, like me, during the period when she was an asylum seeker she was forced to settle for small things because of her status. She did a lot of volunteering before she formed AWEF and FaGee Fashions. Many of the organisations where she volunteered thrived on using her unique story for their own ends.

I was pleased when she set up AWEF and Fagee Fashions and claimed greater control over her destiny. Organisations like the Rayne Foundation and TERN have recognised her leadership and entrepreneurial potential and are now helping her to achieve her goals. Faith has worked hard to develop her organisations. She is 'head-cook and bottle-washer' and needs to do more to develop the capability and capacity of both AWEF and FaGee Fashions so that she is able to delegate effectively and devote more of her own time to strategic planning and management.

Faith is a great asset to her community. She is a strong champion for disadvantaged women. She is always there for them no matter what their needs; whether it is help with asylum and immigration issues, domestic violence, and forced separation from their children, social isolation or financial hardships. AWEF is at the forefront of championing the causes of these women and offering a forum where their voices can be heard. Faith has made tireless effort in moving herself forward and I strongly believe her greatest success is still ahead of her.

Deborah Simon – Business Coach and Associate Lecturer observed that this is a compelling biography of one woman's journey which demonstrates the incredible strength not only to survive but to be a winner in all she sets out to achieve. She summarised her experience with me as follows:

Deborah Simon – Business Coach and Associate Lecturer
I was initially introduced to Faith 11 years ago when I attended a Women's Empowerment Conference, which she organized and hosted. I believe at the time she had not yet secured her refugee status in the UK, but was very much an activist of empowering and supporting other women in a similar position to herself.

Being faced with challenges such as financial instability, rejection, lack of accommodation and even homelessness, Faith continued to be persistent in her pursuits to create financial independence by setting up her own social enterprise FaGee Fashions. Again having to overcome some of the barriers of social stereotyping in her attempts to accessing the funds required to ensure a smoother transition into the world of business, she has succeeded on multiple levels, including creating streams of independence for others and herself.

She has a keen eye to identifying the needs of others, and allowing herself to be a role model and an aid at their disposal, often supporting them with all that she has. It was no surprise when she embarked on her own business she chose a social enterprise business model – with the intention not only to produce and supply affordable products, but to create jobs to assist other women to have financial independence and strategies to move onto the next stage in their journey.

Faith is fearless and has a unique set of talents, skills and passion. She is a woman of influence and strength who has inspired vulnerable women through her example as a leader and entrepreneur. I admire her formidable courage and tenacity. I am proud to call her a friend and colleague.

Kevin Ncube was so impressed with my work that he wrote this poem:

KEVIN NCUBE – (I have written this Poem for my friend Faith Gakanje, who is an exemplary African mother).

Mum you are the communities regal African queen
Your designs captivating, FaGee squeaky clean
For sure, educate a woman
Educate a nation
Your community cohesion ideals keep us keen
In realising your big ideas never before seen.

Mother, you to me are more precious
Than silver and gold
You work your fingers to the bone
Here's hoping you will be rewarded manifold.

The African Women's Empowerment Forum
Only cements your good name and decorum
You continue shriek in unison
With resilience of an African son.

Like the African sun, you caressed my young limbs
With that everlasting motherly love
All your prayers and dedication
Fitted mine like a hand to a glove.

Aluta continua in your plea to say
That practical thank you to Britain
For offering you a home away from home – sanctuary
And helping yield success for certain.

We revere you and all those you work with

A LIFE ROBBED

For you taught me that no man is an island
You have propelled Africa to the very forefront
And made us peacock proud of this land.

I feel forever indebted to you
For giving me faith in life anew
For being Faith loved by all not a few
To you Mama, adulation is surely due.

May you continue to strive
Fruitful activity – just like a beehive
All that genuine nectar
I know you adore your voluntary sector.

So go on, walk the walk – stride
The ramp is yours and so is the lap of honour
Afro-centric, in you we confide
Well-choreographed, well-accessorised.

Batik, chitenge and all the raw material
Audiences will scramble to your fashion serial
Earth colours, traditional headgear
Barefoot, swaying models with no fear.

Deportment, confidence, uniqueness
Mama all the above – and yes
Happiness is your business.

It is no exaggeration to say the testimonials above, as well as the numbers of beneficiaries of African Women's Empowerment Forum (AWEF), demonstrates that empowerment is at the heart of our programme and values.

It is my contention that if asylum seekers are settled timeously, they can contribute to economies of host countries immensely because they all have the potential to do so when an enabling environment has been afforded to them.

CHAPTER EIGHT

REFLECTIONS, LESSONS AND RECOMMENDATIONS

'People who seek protection in the UK should be treated fairly and humanely.'

British Red Cross

This chapter concludes with the key lessons which asylum seekers and refugees can learn from my experience with the UK asylum system. It also contains recommendations for improving the asylum system so that it can better meet the needs of both the policy makers and people seeking sanctuary. At a time when the number of people seeking sanctuary has reached record proportions, governments and other organisations need to ensure their policies to help displaced people are fit for purpose. The scale of the problem can be seen from the following figures. By the end of 2017, statistics compiled by the UN Refugee Agency put the number of people displaced by war and other factors at 68.5 million. This was 2.9 million more than the figure at the end of 2016. Media tends to mislead the public by giving the wrong reasons why people seek asylum; the truth is that most refugees seek protection in neighbouring countries within their region of origin. This is often in developing countries. However, over the past decade the number fleeing to Europe has been steadily increasing. The numbers who seek protection in the UK is low compared to countries like Spain, Italy, Greece and Germany. I decided to share my experiences and the pain and suffering which I endured through the UK asylum process. Everyone has the right to seek asylum. This is a fundamental human right which is written into international law. As an asylum seeker I realised that I was not breaking any laws. Under the 1951 Geneva Convention Relating to the Status of Refugees, all I needed to do was to provide clear and strong evidence to show that I was running away from persecution. Persecution may occur on grounds of your race, religion, nationality, political opinion or membership of a particular social group. I also demonstrated that I was unable to get suitable protection from the authorities in my own country. In such a case, you have the right to stay in the country where you have sought protection while you are awaiting a decision on your asylum application but it took me nearly nine years to be recognised as a refugee.

In this book I have shared areas that I realised asylum seekers might need help with, such as rights and entitlements of asylum seekers, how to communicate their case effectively, and tips on how to integrate in the host society and reduce social isolation. I have also given advice to asylum seekers.

When one volunteers to work with the community, the chances are that one will learn the importance of using time effectively while the asylum claim is being processed, how to budget effectively, and useful sources of help and further information. If I had had this information from the start, my journey of asylum seeking in the United Kingdom would not have taken so many years.

I also realised that, when presenting my case, I was supposed to provide clear written evidence to support it, consistent with my written evidence and any other testimonials which I provided to support my application. Keeping eye contact during conversations or interviews is something I learnt in this country. Perseverance is a virtue. If your application is rejected, you have the right to appeal against the decision. It does not mean you are breaking the law. Your application may have been rejected because you did not present your case effectively. Your refusal letter will normally explain the reason for the rejection of your application and your right to appeal. It will also mention the timescale within which you have to act. Seek advice from your solicitor or a suitable refugee organisation in the area where you are based on how to submit an appeal.

I also realised that I needed to find a suitable asylum network forum in my community and contribute in whatever way I could. It is important to seek as many opportunities as possible to get to know your community, understand the norms, the culture and how things are done. Try and pluck up the courage to introduce yourself to your neighbour.

Attend the local library and find out what free activities are available. Visit a church and get to know people. Try and find an asylum and refugee forum and contribute in whatever way you can. This may mean sharing and celebrating your culture with local people. You will find that many local people are interested in knowing more about your personal journey, your country of origin, language, cuisine, music and other aspects of your culture. That way you will get to know the correct and the right people and places to visit.

I also benefited from a wealth of network of asylum seekers and refugees. These are usually hosted by groups of community organisations, churches and other charities. They offer a wide range of services to welcome and support the integration of asylum seekers and refugees. Services typically include offering information and advice, English language classes, activities for adults and children, health and well-being support, meals and practical help with clothes and other necessities. There are plenty benefits for participating in community activities. You will settle and integrate into the community more quickly. You will improve your language skills and gain a better understanding of the local culture. It is also good for your mental and physical health. If you cut yourself off from the local community, loneliness and social isolation can otherwise damage your health and make it more difficult for you to settle and succeed in the UK.

I also realised that the asylum process can be long and drawn out. When you are in such a situation, you should ensure you have a plan to develop your skills while you are waiting to hear the outcome of your application. The asylum process can be long and protracted. You may find yourself waiting for years for a decision on your asylum claim. During that time you will find it difficult to access education and to gain the right to work. Although in principle you can apply for permission to work if you find yourself waiting for a decision on your case for more than a year through no fault of your own, in practice this is rarely granted.

It is important to have a personal development and well-being plan to stay positive during the waiting period. Don't focus on what you are not allowed to do. Instead focus on what is possible. Seek suitable volunteering opportunities to maintain your skills or develop new skills. In addition, volunteering helps you to learn about your new community. It can help you to integrate and develop vibrant social networks. It is also advisable to access whatever training or educational opportunities are open to you. Usually, these are free so long as you present your Asylum Seekers Card at the time of application and registration.

In my own case, although I was reduced to destitution, I did not give up on leading a fulfilling life. In order to integrate myself into the wider society and get an insight into community work in the UK, I volunteered as a cleaner and shop assistant with the Save the Children charity between the years 2003 and 2005 in Nottingham. Later I volunteered in other organisations like the Refugee Forum, Nottingham City of Sanctuary, Nottingham Black

Partnership, Nottingham Community Voluntary Services, Rainbow Project and the African Women Initiative Support project. During my time with these organisations, I was privileged to work with people from different communities and diverse cultural backgrounds. This experience was what inspired me to establish AWEF. I wanted to be part of the solution to address issues faced by refugees and asylum seekers – especially marginalised African women.

I enrolled with the People's College of Nottingham and studied different courses in order to improve myself academically. I obtained certificates in Access to Nursing, Aroma Therapy, Introduction to Law, First Aid, Food Hygiene and Infection Control. I would have liked to train as a nurse, specialising in midwifery but I was not given the opportunity because of my immigration status. I even enrolled in a Foundation Degree in Community Regeneration and Development at University of Derby. I nearly completed the course. The course enhanced my understanding of issues of equality in a multicultural society. It taught me problem-solving, team-work, networking, organisational development and communication skills.

I also the needed to learn to budget and make the most of my subsistence allowance. As an asylum seeker without children or a spouse, I received an allowance of £36.95 a week or £5.28 per day to live on. The state provided me with accommodation and utilities like heating and electricity. From my weekly allowance of £36.95, I was expected to pay for your food, clothing, toiletries, hairdressing visits, transport, medicine, telephone calls to keep in touch with families back home and other everyday necessities. I learned to budget carefully in order to avoid getting into debt and going without basic needs. I always thought twice before I did any spending. For example, when I was faced with spending on a bus ticket, I considered walking or checked if it was possible to get a lift from someone who drives. I learnt to check prices carefully before buying anything and select the cheaper brands. Most supermarkets offer bargain deals towards the end of each day. I looked out for these reductions and considered buying discounted items for storing in the refrigerator. I also considered making use of food and clothing banks. Charity shops also offer clothes at very good value, sometimes as little as 25 pence per item of clothing. Instead of a mobile phone contract, consider using 'pay as you go' and free Wi-Fi and internet when you are in public places. Places like public libraries, shopping centres and McDonalds offer free Wi-Fi and internet service. This way I was able to save my allowance for emergencies. With careful budgeting, it is possible to save, even from £5 per week. I managed to save from my allowance and this helped me through those lean periods when the government withdrew my benefits. If you are classed as a 'failed asylum seeker', your benefits will be stopped and without savings you will find yourself destitute.

My experience is that you will also need to have savings to fall back on during the transition period if you are granted refugee status. Your allowance will stop at this point and there are delays in obtaining mainstream benefits (Universal Credit). It is also possible that you may become homeless, as you are only given 28 days to vacate accommodation provided to you by the Home Office and find alternative housing. If you are lucky to find a house within the 28 days interval, you are likely to need money or help to furnish it. Many people seeking sanctuary find themselves destitute during the transition period between being an asylum seeker and becoming a refugee. If you master the skill of managing your weekly £36.95 asylum allowance, this will also help you to manage your Universal Credit benefit if you are granted refugee status. Universal Credit is paid as a monthly lump-sum and will require careful management so that you do not run out of money before the month ends.

I also realised that one must be resilient and not to be put off by hostile interviews and rejections. Asylum interviews can be daunting and hostile, especially if the caseworker is not well trained or is in a bad mood. You may find yourself waiting for long periods for a decision on your claim. It took nearly nine years for my case to be decided. I know people who are waiting for 20 years. I kept on fighting until I got a fair outcome. You have the right to seek protection from persecution and harm. Keep on asserting it and remember your rights include the right to appeal against unfair decisions. While you are waiting, do everything you can to look after your health. Don't spend all your time at home in anticipation of a good news letter from the Home Office. The waiting can be frustrating so you need to occupy your time with useful activities.

I also realised the need to ask for help. It is important that you have a good overall understanding of the asylum process from the time you apply for asylum up to the final decision. Seek advice from an immigration solicitor or your local Citizens Advice office. Advice from the Citizens Advice office is free and confidential. If you are a member of a local Asylum and Refugee Forum, they will also be able to help you with any queries or needs you have. At the very least, you can expect them to point you in the right direction. The support of friends and your wider network is also important. They may be able to help you in times of difficulty such as when you have to appeal against a negative decision from the Home Office. They may also be able to provide you with moral and practical support if you become homeless or destitute. There are a number of legal guides provided by private law firms which can also help you to gain better access to information about your rights without you having to rely solely on Home Office guidance. I find the book by Willman, S. and Knafler, S. (*Support for asylum-seekers and other migrants: a guide to legal and welfare rights*. London, Legal Action Group, 2009) to be particularly helpful. This book is very comprehensive and clearly written. I wish I had known about it while I was going through the asylum process.

Recommendations and conclusion

These recommendations I am making are aimed at the Home Office policy makers. I do not recommend an overhaul of the whole asylum system but an improvement in certain areas where service delivery might improve. If accepted, these improvements would help to bring about a fair and fit-for-purpose asylum system which meets the needs of both the people seeking sanctuary and the government. It would lead to a more efficient system where asylum cases are processed quickly and the right decisions are made. At the same time, asylum seekers would be better prepared to settle in the host community and make a bigger social, cultural and economic contribution. There would also be less dependence on state hand-outs and fewer negative outcomes such as physical and mental ill-health, homelessness, destitution, and people absconding and engaging in illegal activities to survive.

Recommendation 1 – The Home Office should conduct a skills audit on all asylum seekers upon arrival.

It is important to compile information about what education, qualifications, skills and experience asylum seekers possess. This information would help the host country to make better use of talents and alleviate labour market problems. It would also help to identify what help asylum seekers need and aid their integration into the local community. A skills audit would empower asylum seekers. It would make clear who they are and what they have to offer the host country in return for protection.

Recommendation 2 – All Local Authorities in the UK should have an integration strategy to welcome asylum seekers on arrival and help them to integrate into the local community.

Integration of refugees should be planned from their first day of arrival to the UK and should be treated as a priority. They should be provided with a Welcome Pack with a coherent integration programme. This should include language training, civic training, labour market activities, such as volunteering, and useful sources of information. They should be given free access to Council-owned gyms and swimming pools. There should also be activities aimed at the local community to welcome asylum seekers. They should be told why we flee here and how we can contribute to the prosperity of the society. Many local people see asylum seekers newly-arrived in their community as dangerous people. If more was done to educate the public and raise awareness about the refugee crisis, this would reduce the discrimination and isolation refugees face.

Recommendation 3 – Asylum seekers should be given the right to work within the first six to twelve months of their arrival.

Asylum seekers are generally banned from working. If their claim has not been processed within a year, they can apply to the Home Office for permission to work but only if they qualify for jobs where there are skills shortages. There is no rational justification for depriving asylum seekers of the right to work. The current policy damages their morale and makes it more difficult for them to settle and integrate into society. It also fosters dependence on state hand-outs and pushes many asylum seekers into destitution. If asylum seekers were allowed to work, money spent on their subsistence could be saved or used to finance other socially worthwhile projects. At the same time, they would be able to make a positive contribution to the economy by meeting areas of skills shortages and paying taxes and national insurance. They would also be able to keep their skills up-to-date.

Recommendation 4 – The Home Office should ensure caseworkers are better trained to assess asylum claims and make decisions more quickly and accurately.

The Home Office decision-making process is long, protracted and fraught with poor judgment. Asylum seekers are often kept waiting in limbo for years and in a large number of cases the wrong decisions are made. The United Nations High Commissioner for Refugees (UNHCR) has found that some Home Office caseworkers do not understand the basics of the law and how to assess applicants' credibility correctly. They do not always take all the evidence supplied by asylum claimants into account; they demand unreasonable supporting evidence from them. The training given to staff should take applicants' cultural practices into consideration. Staff should also be sensitive to the traumas which people seeking sanctuary have gone through before coming to the

UK. This can undermine their confidence and their ability to present their case effectively. It can also lead to memory problems. It is also important for staff to treat asylum seekers with respect and dignity. It is also important that both parties have access to skilled language interpreters if English is not the applicant's mother tongue.

Recommendation 5 – Asylum seekers whose claims have been rejected should retain their subsistence, housing and other support until they are deported.

If your case is rejected, you become a failed asylum seeker and you lose entitlement to your £36.95 a week allowance, your housing and all other forms of support. You are expected to return home voluntarily or you are deported. This treatment is inhumane. Regardless of one's status, one's human rights should be respected. All human beings need to have shelter, food, clothing, healthcare and other basic necessities. This also applies to failed asylum applicants. They have the same needs as those whose applications are under consideration. This policy needs to be changed. It leads to destitution, illegal working, crime and people absconding.

Recommendation 6 – The Home Office should provide better transition support to asylum seekers once they are granted refugee status.

Once refugee status is granted, the current policy is to give asylum seekers a maximum of 28 days to find new accommodation and apply for Universal Credit to replace their asylum allowance. As noted before, this period is not long enough and it often results in many people with refugee status becoming homeless and destitute. They should be given a longer period to find alternative accommodation. Experience shows that three months is a more reasonable period. A recent study carried out by the British Red Cross found that 15,000 refugees and asylum seekers were left destitute in 2017 and had to rely on the Red Cross for emergency food parcels. Almost a quarter (23%) of those seeking food had refugee status[23].

Given delays in obtaining a National Insurance number and processing benefits, the government should also provide those with refugee status with an interest-free refugee integration loan. This would help them with needs such as buying furniture, preparing for education, work or starting a business.

Conclusion

It is my sincere belief that the current regime of hostility does more harm than good. It fails to treat vulnerable and traumatised people with the respect and dignity they deserve. It dehumanises them, drives them into destitution, and damages their mental and physical health. Ultimately, it robs them of their self-esteem and their very life. This is why so many asylum seekers end up self-harming and taking their own lives. Instead of seeing asylum seekers as a burden, governments should see them as a potential asset to the host country. They should be given every chance of protection and settlement. Their asylum claim should be assessed fairly and efficiently, rather than assuming from the outset that they are all bogus applicants.

REFERENCES

ENDNOTES

[1] Lyons, Tanya. *Guns and Guerrilla Girls: women in the Zimbabwean liberation struggle*, Trenton, Africa World Press (2014).

[2] Paton, Alan. *Cry the Beloved Country*, Bennett Cerf, (1948).

[3] Banana, C. S. 'Report of the Workshop on the Role of Women in Social, Economic and Cultural Reconstruction of Zimbabwe – Harare' (1982).

[4] Meredith, M. *The State of Africa – a History of the Continent since Independence*, Simon & Schuster, (London 2005).

[5] McDowell, C. *Breakthrough Britain: Asylum Matters Centre for Social Justice*, (2008).

[6] https://www.theguardian.com/public-leaders-network/2017/apr/08/asylum-caseworkers-home-office-cuts-syria-war

[7] https://www.theguardian.com/uk-news/2018/feb/11/lottery-asylum-system-unjust-home-office-whistleblowers

[8] https://www.refugee-action.org.uk/wp-content/uploads/2018/05/Waiting-in-the-Dark

[9] Joint Committee on Human Rights The Treatment of Asylum Seekers Tenth Report of Session 2006–07. London, Parliamentary Publications (2007).

[10] Home Office Enforcing the Rules: A Strategy to Ensure and Enforce Compliance with our Immigration Laws, London, Home Office (2007).

[11] https://www.theguardian.com/uk-news/2018/aug/17/revealed-asylum-seekers-20-year-wait-for-home-office-ruling

[12] Ibid.

[13] https://www.bbc.co.uk/news/uk-43422787

[14] https://www.independent.co.uk/news/uk/home-news/asylum-seekers-held-removal-centres-home-office-emergency-housing-a8354731.html

[15] https://www.theguardian.com/uk-news/2017/oct/27/uk-asylum-seekers-living-in-squalid-unsafe-slum-conditions.

[16] Zetter, R. and Pearl, M. 'The minority within the minority: refugee community-based organisations in the UK and the impact of restrictions on asylum-seekers', Journal of Ethnic and Migration Studies (2000).

[17] https://www.theguardian.com/world/2014/mar/08/professional-refugees-lawyers-doctors-minimum-wage-uk

[18] https://www.redcross.org.uk/about-us/news-and-media/media-centre/press-releases/press-release-uk-asylum-system-leaving-thousands-of-people-in-poverty

[19] https://www.dailymail.co.uk/news/article-5856117/Four-Eritrean-asylum-seekers-taken-lives-UK-year-coming-Calais.html

[20] Cohen, J 'Safe in our hands: A study of suicide and self-harm in asylum seekers', Journal of Forensic and Legal Medicine (2008).

[21] https://www.mentalhealth.org.uk/statistics/mental-health-statistics-refugees-and-asylum-seekers

[22] https://www.refugee-action.org.uk/wp-content/uploads/2018/05/Waiting-in-the-Dark

[23] https://www.redcross.org.uk/about-us/news-and-media/media-centre/press-releases/press-release-uk-asylum-system-leaving-thousands-of-people-in-poverty